List to Last:

How to Survive Every

Real Estate Market Crash

Ricky Carruth

For Mom and Dad

You taught me to work hard and believe

Zero to Diamond Publishing
Orange Beach, Alabama

List to Last:

How to Survive Every Real Estate Market Crash

Table of Contents

Foreword

When I started the *Zero to Diamond* organization (educational and motivational books, courses, coaching and online resources), I had no idea the response I would get or the impact it would make. I had never coached any agents nor have I ever written a book. All I knew was that the way I sold real estate was unique and special.

•I do not call "For Sale By Owners" or "Expired Listings."

•I don't buy expensive online ads or internet leads from Zillow, Facebook, Google, etc.

•I do not use some "magical" computer program.

What works for me is a method of creating lifelong relationships with property owners who own the type of property I want to sell. The results are second to none. The way I approach every potential client is like family: low-pressure, easy going, hardworking, consistent, professional, dependable, knowledgeable. One thing that sets my approach apart from most is my low-pressure philosophy. I absolutely do not care about pushing a deal with a prospect. My goal is to help that person accomplish exactly what they are trying to accomplish. Not what I want to accomplish. Helping them may not even result in a deal, ever. And that's okay. But they know that I'm real. Authentic. Genuine. Each person can see it in my eyes that I truly care about him or her as a person.

When you genuinely care about people, they will genuinely care about you back.

After publishing my first book, *Zero to Diamond: How to Become a Million Dollar Real Estate Agent*, I was overwhelmed by the 5-star reviews, and by agents who reached out to me telling me how it changed their lives. So this second book is very special to me. I really get into the details of my business and give you a guide to go by that, if used, will produce huge results over time.

Since I started writing and coaching, I have learned a few things. One is that the real estate business is simple. Another is that real estate success is not easy. What I mean is that the fundamentals of success are simple and teachable, but successfully implementing those principles for years and years is *not* easy. Most people want the easy way out.

There is no easy way out.

Success is a grind. You must enjoy the process and the everyday work. If you don't love what you do, you will fail.

Enjoy this book, as I have put my heart and soul into it for you, and I hope you understand that the game of real estate—and life itself—is a journey.

Introduction

If you are a real estate agent who would like to become a better *Listing* Agent, this book is for you. Being a Listing Agent is the most efficient and profitable avenue to success. Don't believe me? Look at the most successful agents out there. Almost all are Listing Agents. Sure, they represent buyers as well, but generally around 80% of their transactions come from listings. And most of the buyers they represent came as by-products of efforts to **list** property, as when an owner/seller also decided to buy, or someone buys one of their listings. So, this book will offer many ways to obtain buyers through concentrating on Listings.

The focus here is on the **advantages** of the Listing side of the real estate equation. For starters, when you gain buyers by way of your listing efforts, they are more informed buyers and thus more efficient to work with. They know what they want and are usually more qualified than a random buyer found online or who came to you from an ad. From every angle, greater success comes from focusing 99% of your efforts on Listings, then taking what buyers come from those efforts. The method of **"Focus on Listings"** is the paved and profitable path to becoming a highly successful agent.

Most Listing Agents did not wake up one day and say to themselves, "Hey! I want to be a listing agent." Nope, few ever had that thought. They *still* may not even consider themselves to be Listing Agents.

Listing Agents are actually just top producers who are extremely good at multiplying their time. It just so happens that obtaining listings is the greatest multiplier of time in the history of real estate. Finding and securing great listings is like franchising yourself.

To illustrate what I mean by *franchising yourself*, let's take one of the greatest franchising stories of all time: McDonald's. When Richard and Maurice McDonalds started out with just one restaurant, they had only one stream of income. They worked (cooked!) very hard every day to just earn the income from one single location. Then Ray Croc convinced the McDonald brothers to start selling franchises. Each franchise they sold was another McDonald's restaurant that opened up in a different location, bringing more income to the original owners. This is a classic case of **multiplying time and ideas**. You know the rest: billions and billions of hamburgers sold, and millions for Croc and the McDonald family —all from a simple idea about how to make bland burgers and fries quickly.

The same process of multiplication can work for real estate agents, especially with listings. Each listing obtained is basically you franchising yourself in different locations over and over again. You do the work to get the listing by prospecting and meeting with potential sellers. Then you find a motivated seller who agrees to list their property with you. You then sign the listing, take pictures, create a great ad and place the property on MLS. Boom! You are done.

Well, not really. But the *hardest* part is done, and of course you must service the listing: handling requests for showings, promoting the property, staying in close touch with the seller about feedback, etc. But these things can be scheduled and some happen automatically when you have the right systems in place.

The bigger point is that once you get the listing, **every agent in your area will be working hard to sell it for you** while you chase other listings. Do you see what is happening here? Two things at the *same time*. Every agent in your area will be trying to sell your listing while you are working hard to find more listings. Since both activities make you money and are happening simultaneously, your time has thus been multiplied. You then have more than one McDonald's restaurant, so to speak.

Top producers understand this concept early on in their careers. They spot it like a sniper spots their target miles away. Once they figure out that listings multiply time like franchising for restaurants, they go *all in*. They focus all their time on finding listings. Once they get one, they throw it in MLS and continue their mission for a huge inventory of listings. They are relentless and quit for nothing or no one. Then they land their second listing. Then a third. They get an offer on one of their listings, and soon it's under contract. Continuing to chase listings, they find another and another. One day they wake up and have a nice inventory of ten to twenty listings or more.

When you concentrate on finding listings and build a solid inventory, the market is working *for* you because you have spread yourself across many listings that other agents are trying to sell. When you work like this, you have the opportunity to pile up deals. Another term for this is *leverage*. Which means you can handle many at one time, lifting them all with one lever.

Conversely, if you only focus on one buyer at a time, showing other agent's listings, you are working *for* the market. Would you rather work *for* the market, or have the market work *for* you? Exactly. It's a no brainer. Of course, some agents could argue that in a similar way, you could pile up a huge list of buyers that could produce plenty of consistent deals over time. But it doesn't work the same way, for a variety of reasons (which we will examine in this book). For starters, you can create a huge inventory of motivated sellers in lightning speed compared to the time it takes to build a buyer database, and you still have to find each buyer the right property. Listings are much easier. You don't have to show property nearly as often (in fact, you may have your assistant arrange for other agents to show your listings).

That is not to say that buyers aren't a wonderful source of income. Remember, Listing Agents should not *call* themselves "just a Listing Agent." They are **dealmakers**. They are top producers who multiply time and facilitate great deals. And they will take a buyer in a heartbeat. They love buyers. The difference is that they do not advertise for, or solicit, buyers. They beat the bushes for listings and if a buyer falls out instead, great. They just don't get as many buyers because they aren't trying to. If buyers were more profitable than sellers, trust me, most successful agents would be categorized as *buyers' agents*.

Most agents can't wrap their mind around only pursuing sellers. They feel like they are leaving all kinds of money on the table if they abandon buyers. So, they spend too much time with buyers, which yields only a few deals here and there. Meanwhile, listing agents have all the time in the world to go after more buyers and sellers because they aren't showing property all day. They spend their time working on huge projects that will create a massive quantity of future listings, while the buyer agents waste too much time working with every random buyer or shopper that comes their way. They have absolutely zero time to think about a project that could create massive future business.

They have a mind block. They have no idea that they are shooting themselves in the foot. They think that by working hard to satisfy everyone, they are on the right path to a high level of success. But instead, they are driving their long-term business in the ground. Blinded by the possibility of a sale, they get caught in a tough situation where potential buyers rule their entire business. After awhile, some of these buyer's agents realize that they are working much harder than listing agents, yet are making less money.

Does any of this sound familiar? Do you know agents like this? Does it sound like you? Agents who work mostly with buyers tell me, "If I turn these buyers down and spend all of my time on sellers, then I am throwing all of that money away." I understand you can't afford to throw money away, but by working with mostly buyers, you are throwing away something more important than money. You are throwing away *time*. Time is more valuable than money. If you lose all your money, you can replace it... but you cannot replace time.

Crossing the fine line between low producers and high producers can only happen when you fully understand the relationship between time and money. This book will show you the philosophies and actions that can enable you to multiply your time. Understand that first. The money will follow.

This business has a way of teasing us into thinking that we are on the right track when we have a deal or two in the works. Don't get me wrong, it's great to have a few deals going, but don't believe that a few deals are worth investing *all* your time in. To be super-successful requires a crazy amount of deals. One, two or even ten deals are a short-term, thumbnail sketch of the big picture you are trying to paint. Sure, spend some time on current deals, but the rest of your time should be multiplied via projects that create the potential for hundreds of future transactions. Projects that generate listings include post-card or flyer mail-outs, prospecting, social media, mass emails and cold calling. Plant seeds for relationships now through massive projects that will yield an abundance of transactions later. Always have a huge marketing project in the works and do your deals on the side. Concentrate on the *activities* that create listings and sales, not the closings themselves.

In this book, **I will take you step-by-step through the process of transforming yourself into a power-selling listing agent who outpaces the competition.** We will talk about building relationships; first, gain trust, then gain business. We will learn how to align ourselves with the right potential clients, which can be the difference in succeeding and barely surviving. And more.

When it comes to actual effort and time invested, there is very little difference between an agent who makes $150,000 a year and one who makes $750,000 a year. The main difference is in philosophy and approach! In my research and studies, I have found that the agent making under $100,000 annually is working just as hard or harder as the agent making $750,000. Hartley Peavey, the founder of the billion-dollar musical instrument company of the same name, said these famous words: "Work smart, not hard." But I'd say, "Work hard *and* smart!"

I see the difference all the time with scenarios of small production vs. huge production and *not-so-smart* vs. *hard-working smart*. Comparing the two agent's business models, I find some interesting facts, such as this one: the lower producing agent has on average only 15% of the number of active listings that the higher producer has. Another is that the lower producing agent spends most of their time trying to satisfy buyers, while the other agent refers buyers out to buyers' agents.

Also, the higher producing agent has a high-quality assistant (and may have had to hire and fire several assistants to find the very best one that fits their business model). The lower producing agent either has no assistant or has a low-quality assistant (but won't replace them). Tentative buyers and a bad assistant will drive your business into the dirt.

You must protect your career by watching out for those things. Sidestep those critical obstacles ahead of time. Sure, it's okay to work tons of buyer leads at the beginning of your career. This gives you much-needed experience. However, through those experiences, the future top producers begin to realize where their time is best spent.

Many mistakes are made in the early stages. This is part of the process. Learn from those mistakes and pay attention to the way real estate works. If you can't learn from your experiences and adjust your business daily to get better, you will have a hard time progressing higher.

Look around at the agents who have made it. Pay attention to them. What are they doing? How are they doing it? Clone their actions and you should also succeed at a high level. Knowing that so many agents have made it in this business should give you the faith that you can as well. All it takes is hard work and a smart allocation of your time. Be efficient. Make sure that everything you do is the most profitable activity at any given moment.

I want you to be as successful as you can and grow to your full potential in real estate and in life itself. If there is anything I can ever do for you, please contact me at www.ZeroToDiamond.com, where you can find a variety of real estate coaching programs for all levels and budgets.

I will call you directly to help you develop a personalized business plan that will take your real estate business to the next level and beyond.

Follow me online:

Facebook: @zerotodiamond

Facebook Group: Zero to Diamond-Real Estate Agents

Instagram: @rickycarruth & @zerotodiamond

Snapchat: @rickycarruth

YouTube: www.youtube.com/c/rickycarruth

Tune in LIVE each week on the Facebook Group for my Real Estate Q&A show, #AskRickyLive.

Subscribe to my YouTube channel for my vlog series, Ricky Carruth's Daily Grind. It's a look inside my daily life and business.

You can also join my weekly email list by texting **"LISTTOLAST" to 22828**.

As a full-time agent, my success has always been measured by how much I help others succeed. So, I look forward to helping you as well. Please know that I care about each and every one of you deeply.

Enjoy.

Chapter 1: When the Market Crashes

In 2005, my world came crashing down.

The economy had weakened, but on the Gulf Coast, the real estate market really started to plummet. This took me by surprise. It came out of nowhere with no warning.

I had built what I thought was a huge, sustainable real estate business. I had been steadily selling properties and investing in properties. The real estate boom of 2003-2004 was my first go around having any significant "extra" money to invest, so I had no experience with exactly what to do with it. I had always heard, growing up in a beach area with rising property values, that real estate was a smart investment. So naturally, I started putting my savings into properties. I had also been told that one should take some risks and "leverage" investments by borrowing. To buy better investment properties, I borrowed on top of my own money. Thus, when the market crashed, I couldn't sustain the payments and was forced into losing every single penny I had. I thought I had been making the right moves to build a big future. It was a mistake… if for no other reason, because of the bad timing.

That disaster was an extreme eye-opener for me. With everything gone, I left real estate and went back into roofing houses for a living. If you've ever lugged an eighty-pound pack of shingles up a ladder in 100-degree heat and Alabama humidity, you know what real work is! I was relieved to land a better-paying job on an oil rig in the Gulf. But that is not easy work either. These were some of the hardest years of my life.

As with many success stories, it was during those hard times that I achieved the most personal growth. During my off time from the sweat and labor, I spent my time reading, reflecting and researching. What did I research? Many things. For one, I took a hard look back through the last few years of my life where I had made a million dollars within a few years, and then shockingly lost every penny. I contemplated my mistakes and pondered what I could have done differently.

Something else I researched: other real estate agents. I started watching closely the other agents in my market, both those who survived the crash and those who were forced out of the business. I especially kept a close eye on the ones who were able to continue selling real estate successfully during that time. I watched their listings and sales, and observed how the market prices, transactions and other market factors fluctuated.

I read over a hundred books on self-development, success-skills, motivation and real estate.

After three years of heavy research and reading, I felt that better days were near, and that I would come back to real estate stronger than ever. It was just a matter of time. I just had to figure out exactly what I did wrong and devise a full proof business plan to dominate my chosen market.

So, that is exactly what I did.

In 2008, the national economy crashed even further, and I was eventually laid off from the oil field. In a way, this turned out to be fortuitous; it forced me back into real estate. The massive actions (my 3 R's: reading, reflecting and researching) during the tough times launched me back into successful realty sales. Even as I was losing my job as a roughneck on the oil rig, I had lined up two pending sales. These two sales were the beginning of an incredible journey back up the mountain.

Thus began my second chance at real estate. Despite the Great Crash of 2007-2008, I was undaunted. Conditioned and experienced, I now had nothing to lose and nowhere to go but UP. I took everything I had learned from my mistakes and failure and turned them into the positives that transformed my career and life into something great.

So what did I learn? What were the mistakes? And what actions did I take with this new knowledge? How would I secure my career against losing everything in the next market crash?

The answers—everything I learned during that time—are all found in the following chapters. Please take this information seriously. This book is not about some sales gimmick, or some "get rich quick" scheme, and not just a way to get you to join my awesome coaching program. (My online university and coaching programs ARE great and I would LOVE for you to consider them… but that is not the point of this book!)

Everything in this book comes from the tried and true methods that have been the pillars of my success. I give it to you on a silver platter for you to soak up and execute. I want you to create whatever kind of real estate business you want. Maybe you are okay with $100,000 per year. Great! Maybe you want $1,000,000 a year. Okay, fine—it's time to get to work.

Before I get into the details of the mindset and the fundamentals, I want to first explain to you exactly how to prepare and survive a market crash based on everything I learned during previous crashes. (I actually endured three crashes: a regional real estate crash of 2005; the national Financial Crisis of 2007-2008, which almost led to another Great Depression; the oily beach disaster of the BP Deepwater Horizon Oil Spill of 2010, which hit my hometown as hard or harder than any place on the Gulf of Mexico.)

First off, understand a few things: Markets will crash sooner or later. It's inevitable. It's like Mother Nature: some rain must fall. A crash in your market may happen next year. Maybe in five years. Maybe ten. If you're lucky, maybe not until twenty years from now. Who knows? Just so I am clear about this, please understand that I am **not** predicting a market crash. Nor the end of the world. If it were my choice, I would like the market to stay right where it is at this very moment, forever. It is a very healthy market, in my opinion. Inventory is on the low side, but that motivates buyers. Interest rates are low. Everyone is happy. But if history is any guide, at some point, things will crash (or at least, decline). And when your market crashes, I want you to be fully prepared for it so that you may thrive even during the crash and recover stronger than ever.

After a downturn, you must take advantage of the recovered market while it lasts and prepare for the next crash coming. The strategies I am about to share with you will work in good times and bad. They will not only carry you through a down market, but also will help you gain more market share as the market recovers. This way, you will be more of a dominating force in the long run.

Another sobering fact that I want you to face is the high number of agents in the U.S. As I write, we are currently at 2.2 million realtors nationwide. This is a 50% increase in the last two years. The inflow of new agents has been a result of this incredible market run we are on. When the market is good, everyone wants in. Right? But another incredible stat is that 80% of real estate agents do not make it through their first three years in the business, and are forced back into working a 9-5 job. With that being said, it will be very interesting to watch what happens over the next few years with these 700,000 brand-new agents. Even if the market continues upward, in theory, 80% of these new agents will quit the business. And more new agents will still try to get into the business. However, if the market crashes, we will see a huge number of agents who get out of the business. And, like I said, the downturn of the market is coming sooner or later.

So, how do you become one of the fortunate agents

who survive the competition and a possible (inevitable?) market crash? What exactly did I learn from the disasters of 205-2010? Well, if I had to sum it all up simply into one word, it would be *relationships*.

In the first phase of my career, the market was so overly good that I didn't have to have or maintain relationships with my clients. I could do deals and walk away from the relationship because so many other deals were right there in front of me. So there was no such thing as past clients for me. It was all new clients, and there were plenty of them.

But when the market crashed, I crashed. I had no relationships in place with anyone, thus nothing to fall back on. This book will dive into the details about building and maintaining relationships with property owners (and more), but for now I want to specifically give you to exact tools to use during a market crash. These tools will help you build your business during a crash regardless of how long you have been in the business. Even if you start in real estate the day the market crashes, it's okay.

When the market starts to crash or decline, the first thing you must do is acknowledge that it is **changing**. Absolutely do not try to pretend that it is not changing. Recognize the change and adapt your business. You will know the market is changing through a variety of signs. Buyers disappear, sellers are nervous, the number of transactions declines, prices go lower, and everyone's general attitude starts to darken. Observe changes in the market and get ready.

Once you face reality and realize you are in a declining market, it's time to change your tactics. You may notice other agents starting to get out of the business. Don't let that create fear in you. Consider it a good thing for yourself because you could pick up more market share during a crash. There will be fewer agents in the market, so more potential properties per agent. As the market recovers, your goal will be to maintain your share of the market, and then your business will boom.

So what exactly do you do when the market crashes? First, call every single past client you have and make sure they are completely (but calmly) informed of the situation and find out if there is anything you can do for them. That is first and foremost. After that, you call every property owner you can who owns a piece of property that you would like to sell. There are an unlimited amount of these owners, so you will never be able to call them all in a million years. So there are no excuses about not having anything to do, or that you don't know *what* to do. I am telling you exactly what to do! Spend every second taking action. Even in a down market, opportunity is unlimited. If you fail, it's because you don't want it bad enough. The recipe to success is very simple. Call owners.

Now, while the market is crashing all around us, what do we say to property owners who are strangers to us, who we have never talked with? This is simple. You can use one of my phone scripts to introduce yourself and make small talk. But at the end of the call, the purpose is to find out which of the three types of property owners they may be during the market decline. All property owners during a market crash will still fall into one of the following groups:

1) Those who must sell because they are in trouble.

2) Those who want to buy because prices are so good.

3) Those who just want to hold on and ride the crash out.

These are the three scenarios property owners are in during a down market. It is your job to contact as many as humanly possible, and find out which of the three categories they fit. With fewer agents and huge opportunities for bargains during a crash, can be a real gold mine for real estate agents. Another way to view it: a crash creates real estate turmoil, but *turmoil* means *turnover*, and for realtors, that still represents potential sales.

With each contact, find out if they have a relationship with another agent, and if not, begin a relationship with them regardless of which of the three groups they are in. If they want to buy in this down market, help them. If they need to sell, help them. If they want to hold on and ride it out, encourage them. Be a positive voice in negative times. Help them all by collecting their email addresses and becoming an information provider to them every week about the market, forever. This will help you maintain a strong relationship with each owner you encounter.

To simplify, I learned that creating and maintaining relationships is the true key to a sustainable, long-term real estate business. However, I learned much more than that as I watched the market crash with my own two eyes and lost everything I had worked for. I learned that agents leave the business and leave tons of market share on the table for the agents who persevere. Over time, the surviving agents' businesses explode tenfold when the market recovers.

I have observed that a relationship-based business grows in an up market and in a down market, so you really don't have to do things much differently as the market changes, except recognize it is changing and stay on top of the situation by alerting your past clients and pushing for new owners to do business with you. A crash will create situations for current owners to buy, sell, or hold, and most importantly, opportunities for you to build stronger relationships because you will be a voice of calm confidence in the tempest.

Confidence does not mean cocky carelessness. Admittedly, we sail through the straits of Scylla and Charybdis, between being too "safe" and pessimistic on one side, and being too cavalier with our cash on the other. Just be mindful of both extremes. But do not be paralyzed by caution. As stated, I am **not** predicting or hoping for a market crash. But when the inevitable happens, whenever that may be, I will not be ruled by fear. I will be more than ready to take action, to retain as much market share as possible, to support and encourage the people around me, and to stack up deals left and right… because I have been through it before and understand how to steer through the storm. Crashes, like storms, don't last forever. They pass.

I hope you remember this strategy and use it when the time is right. It will help you bypass the heartache of losing everything you have and returning temporarily to a lesser job. You may not be as lucky as me. You may not get a second chance in real estate if you don't survive a crash. Give it everything you have. If you understand what this chapter is saying, then you should have confidence in your ability to cope and adapt… so you don't care if the market crashes or not! You are a real estate agent for life.

Whether good times, bad times, or middlin' times, the rest of this book will cover in detail exactly how to build, maintain and grow your business, based around becoming a listing agent foremost, and a "relationship agent" forever.

Chapter 2: The Mindset of the Listing Agent

Before you become a listing agent, you must **think** like a listing agent. It all starts in your mind before it grows into action. Believing you can do it is the first step, as simple as that sounds. But the belief has to be more than just a passing thought or an unconvincing "Maybe I can do it" or "I hope I succeed." It must be a confident "I know I can!" Plenty of agents make it this far, but then never take the next solid step. It may seem strange to call a thought "solid," but true belief requires a solid, confident, defined commitment, connected with and followed by a concrete action-step.

A successful agent is always moving forward, asking themselves, "What's the next step? What's the next piece of the puzzle? How do I get better?" Real estate is 80% mental and 20% physical. Win the war in your mind and you will win the war of success. Believe in yourself with such confidence that nothing will hold you back from achieving your goals to becoming a bona fide Listing Agent.

Once you have the confidence and motivation, it's time to find the next puzzle piece. You will see other agents with 20, 30, 50 or even 100 listings. So, you know it's possible. Now it's your time to step up to the plate. Do the things that most agents are not willing to do, such as making phone calls and setting appointments. Real estate is a human resources business. Contacting and effectively communicating with as many human beings as possible is the name of the game.

Of course, most of your communication should be with potential clients. But also start talking to the top-producing agents in your market about how they conduct their business. Some will give you great information. Especially note when the top-producing agents have successes, and mimic their activities. Watch their numbers and how they line their success up with their daily habits. What time do they come to work? What time do they leave? What do they do when they get to the office? What do they do all day? By paying attention to what the top producers are doing —and asking questions about it—you'll begin to get more of an idea of their habits. Then start incorporating the same habits into your routine.

After a little research and observation, you may realize that what they do is not that difficult. They work hard, contact people all day long, build great relationships on trust, and concentrate on obtaining well-priced listings. The difference between you and them is that they have been very consistent with these actions for years or decades.

Take a moment and picture yourself as the number one listing agent in your area. Think about how good it feels to reach the top. Let this feeling sink in as you ponder your future. You can do this. It is inside of you. It's inside of everyone. All agents can reach their goals —if their *mind* allows them to reach their full potential. **Don't allow your mind to tell you that you can't do it, or that you aren't talented enough.** The truth is that everyone has talents that other people do not. Everyone can connect with people in one way or another.

What is your special talent? How many connections are you willing to make? Making one connection is easy. Making thousands is hard. But the *process* for each connection is the same. You repeat the same actions over and over. Some agents stop at one connection, some at one hundred. Others never stop connecting with people, ever. They reach a thousand connections and keep going. Agents who never stop connecting with both past and new clients will always thrive under any market condition. Make it a habit and focus on it.

It goes beyond the initial call. To understand it best, think of your business like building a brick wall. You want the wall (your business) to be as strong and tall as possible. Each new prospect that you connect with is a single brick that is added to the wall. If you stay in touch with that prospect and help them with future deals and ask for referrals, that brick stays intact. If you do not stay in touch with them, it's the same as the brick crumbling into dust. Then your wall falls.

So, when building your wall, remember two things: you must maintain the old bricks that make up the foundation of the wall, and you must have a consistent supply of new bricks to add the top. This is where staying in contact with people maintains a strong foundation, and consistent prospecting for new clients builds your wall taller. You must do both to build a great wall. The agent who builds the strongest, tallest wall dominates their market and the competition.

Multiply Your Time

If you want to think like a listing agent, there are several areas you should focus on. Listings agents have different theories that they live by. All their decisions are rooted in these theories or principles. The first principle is **multiplying time**. Listing agents are very time-oriented... they are "time freaks," if you will. They understand that time is more valuable than money and that it should be treated as such.

This means making decisions around what saves time and energy. Decisions that result in higher production usually have a way of multiplying time. Do things today that save time tomorrow.

There are two parts to multiplying your time.

- Thinking Speed
- Putting Systems in Place

Listing agents are always working at a very fast pace. This is because, in their mind, they are always in a time crunch. This may sound silly to low producers because the high producers make so much money and are always way ahead of schedule. Low producers don't understand why they are in such a hurry all the time. The truth is that high producers feel like they are in a time crunch not in the short term, but in the *long term*. They know that they are on time to the next meeting and are doing great in the overall scheme of things. But they are also in a race to meet their yearly goals and even next year's goals. That's how far ahead they think. And they act like they are behind on those goals. They know that every decision, each step and every second of each day will determine if they hit their goals or not. One false move could prevent them from achievement. This mental approach motivates them to always work at a high pace. On the outside, it seems that they are doing very well for themselves and shouldn't be in such a hurry to do more business. But this sense of urgency is what separates the high producers from the low.

High producers have goals that most people never imagine. They are willing to do whatever it takes to achieve those goals. Low producers don't understand the urgency as they slowly work on one or two deals. Multiply your time by refusing to obsess over one or two deals. Get in a hurry to put together another ten or twenty deals. Having one or two deals going on should give you a sense of urgency—because that is a very low number. We are looking for actions that create hundreds of future deals. This is what creates a high producer.

When you think speed, think about closing the gap between each action. For example, when you are making phone calls, don't waste time in between calls. As soon as the conversation is over, start dialing the next phone number. Do not pause between calls to check emails or do research. These are just distractions and excuses not to make another call. Listing agents are goal oriented. If making fifty calls in one sitting is the goal, they won't stop dialing numbers until they reach fifty calls. Pursue the calls one after another as if you were in the biggest hurry imaginable.

High producers know that one small distraction could prevent them from finishing. They turn off their emails and close their door. They leave no room for error. They maximize every second they have. For example: get to work early and start promptly on your routine. Listing agents start working early and when they start, it's like a wild man (or woman). Most high-producing agents do more work before 10 am than some agents do all week: planning, emailing, calling, researching. They waste no time. They come in and work every minute until they either have an appointment or lunch. They leave for their appointment with just enough time to get there on time. Then after the appointment, they rush right back to the office and start right where they left off, resuming whatever money-making activity or project is on the list.

Thinking *speed* multiplies your time in a fashion that enables you to accomplish ten times more than anyone else. Be on top of your game and have purpose. Plan your next move always. Know what you are going to do before you do it. Take a few minutes at the beginning and end of each day to plan your day. Map out exactly what you need to do over the next 24 hours to be the most successful. This way, when you come to the office the next day, you will already have your actions planned and can get started blowing past the other agents around you. Have confidence that they cannot outwork you and that you will contact more people and create more results than anyone.

The second part of multiplying your time is to **have great systems in place**. Smart, efficient systems are a huge part of buying more time and productivity. For example, having systems in place that take care of administrative activities —almost automatically—gives you more time to concentrate on the monetary activities. Systems can include many things. A quick, tiny example: set up your bills on auto-pay so you don't have to think about them. Once you have a steady income stream, a big part of your system will include hiring a great assistant to handle all the processing and advertising of your business. It could be having past clients advocate for your business and refer you to lots of potential buyers and sellers.

The point is to put productive systems in place throughout your business that save you time and energy and which also produce higher results in the long run. Implement anything that will enable you to concentrate purely on the activities that make you money, like prospecting, meeting with clients, listing appointments, showing property, negotiating contracts, going to closings, etc. If you notice, all money-making activities involve either communicating or meeting with people. Staying in front of *people* should be 95% of your time spent. Everything else needs to have a system in place that takes those pressures off your shoulders.

Focusing your business around *obtaining listings* is key to multiplying your time. **Listings are the greatest multiplier of time in the history of real estate.** Think about this for a minute. This is very important. When you get a listing and put it into MLS, all other agents in your area see it immediately and start trying to sell it for you.

This gives you time to chase more listings while other agents are working hard to sell the ones you already have.

The concept of obtaining great listings and multiplying your time is the quickest way to high production and consistent closings. Use it! This is the real estate gods' great gift to you. Here's an opportunity to build lifelong relationships with thousands of property owners, obtain hundreds of listings from these relationships, and provide plenty of time to focus on these relationships... while other agents are out there working as hard as they can to sell your listings for you. Your job is to get the listings at the right price and commission as well as create a great online advertisement for the property. Getting great listings to multiply your time is another form of a system that you are putting in place in your business that buys you time to create more business. Don't let this opportunity pass you by. Become extremely listing oriented and only take buyers that come from your listing efforts and referrals.

Think Quality

"Think speed until you are in front of a potential client. Then think quality." -Ricky Carruth

Speed is great, and that is what gets you the *quantity* of relationships you need to reach your goals and beyond. However, **speed is only used in between actions, not *inside* actions.** Early in the process, when we are making calls, we want to go after goals (numbers/speed). For example, when we are making calls, we want to go from one call to another as quickly as possible so that we can make more calls. However, once we get a prospect on the line, everything slows down and **quality becomes our aim**. This is only during the call. Once the call is over, we are back to thinking speed again, until we get another prospect on the phone. During the call, we want to slow down and pay complete attention to the conversation with that prospect. We want to find out what their real estate and life goals are and how we can help them achieve those goals. If there is a deal to be made today, we want to help them with that. If there is not a deal to be made today, we want to make a strong connection with them, exchange contact information and stay in touch with them for future deals. Go above and beyond to let them know that you are here for them and are more interested in helping them than doing a real estate transaction. Focus on their goals and motivations and you will win them over as their agent when the time comes to buy or sell.

When you show up to a listing appointment or to show property to a buyer, think of them as your last client on earth. Give them quality attention. Nothing matters except them during your time together. Sure, work all the way up to the meeting as hard as you can, accomplishing big things, and head to the meeting with just enough time to get there, and after the meeting, hurry back to add to your incredible accomplishments of the day. But *while you are with the client*, spend as much time as they need, never rush them and focus 100% of your mind on them and their needs. Leave your phone in the car. Do not answer your phone or check messages while meeting with a potential client. Have all the necessary information printed out and researched for them. You want them to know that even as busy of an agent as you are, they still have your undivided attention during the entire meeting. This will make a huge impression on them and a very strong bond between you will be created. This is what we are looking for. Transactions come and go, but relationships are forever. And a relationship is far more valuable than anything else.

So to recap: multiply your time by thinking speed and setting up systems in your business. However, while you are thinking speed and getting from client to client, when you finally do get them on the phone or meet them in person, think quality. Put them first over everything else. Show them that they are important to you and that you genuinely care about seeing them accomplish their goals. This is how a listing agent thinks and acts. This is how they become a high producer. It is up to you to start thinking, acting and producing like a top selling listing agent.

Focus on the Big Picture

Take a minute and think about your future. Imagine yourself ten and twenty years from now. Where will you be and what will you be doing? Are you successful? Are you helping people through charities and good business? Are you happy? Have you achieved your goals? This is the big picture. Thinking long-term. This is what the listing agent, or high producer thinks about, using these thoughts to drive their actions and decisions every second of the day. The big picture is the long-term view of both your life and business. It embodies a *why* for your goals as well.

When you create goals and think long-term, you must have your *why* in place as a reason and driver towards your goals. *Why* are you doing this? Why do you want to achieve great success? What are you trying to really accomplish? These are some of the questions you should be asking yourself. Everyone's "Why" is different. Maybe your "Why" is that you want to provide a better life for your family. Maybe it's because you want to become a huge contributor to a specific charity, or to make a difference in your community or the world. Maybe you want a nicer house in a nicer area with better opportunities for your children. Maybe you have sick parents you need to take care of. Your "Why" is for you to choose. But you must have a "Why" in place. You must know the reason you are doing this. Once you realize your "Why", use it as a driving force behind your business, to push yourself to work harder and smarter every minute. Your ultimate goal, vision and inspiration will sustain you through hard time. Without a clear "Why," you will not have the unshakeable determination it takes to survive in real estate.

With the failure rate so high in this industry, you are basically trying to defy gravity. You are trying to do the impossible and beat the statistics. This is a tough task to take on, especially if you are a new agent with zero experience. Only two out of ten new agents make it through their first few years. You need every advantage and opportunity one can find. Start by finding your "Why." Without that in place, you will not have the high level of motivation you need to start moving in the right direction. Your "Why" needs to be a clear, written statement that conveys your burning desire, a desire which fuels you to push past any distractions or obstacles in your way.

So much of this business is mental. Having the right mindset, making decisions around that mindset and staying on course will determine your future. If you only incorporate a vague mindset around just "making money," you will not be successful. Your mindset must be about building great relationships and having systems in place to create and maintain those relationships over the life of your career.

I hope this chapter has opened your mind to how a listing agent thinks and acts. It is very important to understand. It could be the difference between success and failure. The good news is that your success is up to you.

Chapter 3: The Myth of Lead Conversion

You hear it all the time from everybody, from brokers, trainers, coaches, even other agents: they all preach **lead conversion**. Let me explain. Lead conversion refers to the rate of prospects (potential clients) that you Close. In other words, out of all the prospects you receive, your lead conversion rate is the percentage of contacts that actually bought or sold a property with you. Everyone wants to show you how to increase your lead conversion rate. They are concerned with, "How can we sell a larger percentage of the leads that we receive?" Although there is value in converting leads and following up, at the end of the day, thinking of lead conversion rates as critical is a mistake. It is not the key to success.

In real estate, your conversion rates will always be low. The low percentage may frustrate you, especially if you are banging your head against a brick wall trying to figure out a magical way to increase it. Listen: **lead conversion is not the problem**. You can't spend your time trying to convert every lead you get. This steals time you could spend on other things—such as filling up your pipeline with more leads. If you have more leads than you can handle, then the conversion rate doesn't matter! If you are successful at generating lots of leads (which means *relationships*), then your conversation rate will be low. But so what? It will be low either way. Why not take massive action to find *more* leads, fill your pipeline up, and then the smaller conversion rate won't matter because the real number of actual closed deals will still be much higher.

For example, if you are proud to have an average conversion rate of 10%, and you have only 20 leads, you'll spend a lot of time and effort on those 20 leads everyday trying to convert them—but in the end, you likely will only get two (10%) closed deals out of it. Good job! But suppose instead you'd spent less time following up on those 20 leads and more time finding *more* leads.

Let's say you found 80 more leads in the same amount of time because you didn't spend as much time fretting over each lead. Sadly, you may think, your conversion rate thus drops to 7%. Now you have 100 leads in the same amount of time, but even at a 7% conversion rate, you now produced 7 deals (not just 2)! Additionally, it provides you with the possibility of a hundred new relationships for future transactions and referrals. Conversion rates alone neither measure last month's profits, nor do they measure the *future* deals those extra contacts may yield.

The above example is a real-life scenario that agents go through every day. Some agents put the same amount of energy into trying to convert the leads they already have that other agents use to find massive amounts of additional leads. Both agents work just as hard, but one produces 2 deals while the other produces 7 —with more future upside. Who wins? Do you see my point? Lead conversion is a myth.

Do not waste time trying to figure out a magical formula for converting leads. But I am not saying, "Do not follow up." Do your best to follow up and help your prospects in every way possible. If there is a deal to be had, go for it. But don't worry about trying to convert every last one of them. Instead focus on getting more leads. More leads solve all problems. Are you not selling enough property? Get more leads. Not enough income? Get more leads. Trying to get out of a slump? Get more leads. Agents who do not succeed in real estate usually have one thing to blame: they failed to get enough leads. This is the number one reason why agents fail. Not because no one would do a deal with them, not because of market conditions, and not because of bad luck. Nope. It is because *they did not do what they needed to do to secure the amount of leads needed to succeed.*

The more leads you have the more closings you will have... it's not rocket science. Leads solve everything. Conversion rates may always be low regardless of what we do. Since you now know that, why not go get a small percentage of a big number of leads instead of a small percentage of a low number of leads?

Look: you have to make it happen. Your success is entirely in your hands. Are you going to step up and use this information to do what you need to do to succeed? Or are you going to get a few leads and spend most of your time on them instead of finding more leads, just hoping and wishing they'd buy something? You must become a lead generating machine.

How? Read my first book! As I advised in my previous book, **come to the office and get on the phone**. Practice the scripts found on my website, www.zerotodiamond.com. Find property owners to talk to about buying and selling real estate. The more leads you get, the less you will be worried about conversion. Fill up your pipeline. Create a great follow-up system (e.g. a weekly email report). The amount of leads that you need right now is so large that you can't even imagine it. It's so big that it would take you years of hard work to obtain if you were working 10 hours a day, 7 days a week. If you are not, in some sense, a lead-finding machine, you will not earn enough to stay in real estate.

New agents grossly underestimate how many leads they need. They also underestimate their potential to get those leads. Don't let the numbers discourage you, but do realize that you are fighting an uphill battle the moment you get your real estate license. You need hundreds of leads—yesterday—to make a living. You need thousands of leads to be Top Producer. Get to work!

Think about the number of agents that fail in this business. Astonishing, isn't it? It is just mind-boggling. Failure is much more than an epidemic in the industry. It's an outright nightmare. We are living in a time when the average real estate agent does not see past their first year of selling. They then have to fall back to an average job, making an average (as in, low) paycheck, living paycheck to paycheck, bill to bill. You must rise above this. Do not reduce yourself to just being average. Get thirsty. Get hungry for success. Become obsessed about it. Eat, sleep and breathe success.

Seek knowledge and sustain motivation. Become empowered by other successful agents in your market. And no matter what, do not compare yourself to the other agents around you who have just started or who don't sell very much at all. The reality is that most of them will not be agents next year. So, you cannot compare yourself to them. Do not settle. That is why so many agents do not make it. They get into the business and follow suit with the rest of the agents just starting out around them —and they all fail. Realize this and do not go down the same path as the rest of them. Go against the grain and shoot for market domination immediately. Do not wait on the other agents to start. Take the lead. Get on the phone with hundreds of possible leads and cause a market disruption. Take control of your market because you want to take control of your life and career.

Here let me add a caution: don't lose your focus by spending too much time reading every book or watching every You-Tube real estate guru. The amount of information available to real estate agents is nearly unlimited. Real estate training, advice and how-to videos are everywhere you look. Real estate is the most informed industry… with the lowest success rate! That is an amazing paradox. Why is this so? Much of the information out there is low quality. For new agents, it's hard to filter through the bad to find the good. So, they try to listen to it all, only to be overwhelmed. After going in a hundred directions, they end up never succeeding at any. You can't start out like a gunslinger in the Wild West, shooting at every shiny penny you see. Have you ever heard the saying, "You can't be a master of one trade if you are a jack of all trades?" It means that if you try too many different ideas at once, you will never master any of them.

To become a top-producing agent, you must master a few things. So be careful what you listen to, read and follow. Be on guard against all the bad information out there. Get to work and decide for yourself what works and what does not. Put everything you have into that one idea that works for you; focus on one or two things that bring you the most business, and quit wasting time on the things that do not. Jesus once said, "You are worried and troubled about many things. But [only] one thing is needed" at any given moment. Once you find what works for you, take that and go crazy. As you gain momentum, don't stop.

To recap: remember that more leads equal more closings… regardless of the conversion rate. So, go for it! This single idea will be the reason that you either fall in line with the mediocre agents who are on their way out of the business, or fall in line with the agents who are on their way to the top. You have the potential to sell millions of dollars in property. See it in yourself and become obsessed with reaching it. This is your time to shine. Grab yourself a small piece of a big pie instead of a small piece of a small pie.

Success is right there in front of you. It is in front of everyone. It all comes down to if you want it or not. There are two kinds of agents in real estate: the agents that go get what they want, when they want it, and the rest of them, many who will become "ex-agents." Which group of agents will you become a part of? You must decide. Take what is yours. Become obsessed. Keep focused, keep pushing forward and reach for the sky.

Chapter 4: Losing Deals

One thing I want you to know up front that will help you tremendously is this: losing deals is an unavoidable part of this game. Of course, do everything you can to secure the deal. Do not take it for granted whatsoever. But, at the same time, accept the fact that you will not win them all. Think about sports: has there ever been a National Champion who first, earlier in their career, had not experienced a loss? Champions hate losing. But they get over it quickly and move on to the next challenge, the next victory.

Losing is part of winning. Maybe you had a listing appointment with a seller who was interviewing three agents, but in the end, he picked another agent. Or maybe you had a property under contract, moments from closing, and it fell through because of an unexpected glitch in financing or inspection. Maybe you had a buyer who just got cold feet. Maybe you showed a particular buyer houses for three straight days and after all of that, they just learned their company is transferring out of state. So no deal. Whatever the case may be, it happens. Losing possible deals is part of this business that you must embrace.

When it happens, the first move to make is to do everything we can do to keep it together. Ask yourself, "Realistically, is there any creative way to overcome the obstacle that blocks us from sealing the deal?" If the obstacle or problem is in an area you lack expertise, then ask someone who is an expert in that arena. They may have an unexpected solution. If the expert tells you, "No, there's really no way around that problem," and you and your client have no other options, it is time to face facts. It's just a dead deal.

After you admit a deal is dead, remember it is not truly worthless. At least **three things remain alive and valuable in a so-called "dead deal":**

1. Hopefully, that client sees how hard you worked for them and eventually, when their timing or circumstance or financing gets right, they will return to you for future business.

2. That client—buyer or seller—may still give you referrals (remember our foundational principle: "It's about relationships").

3. You learned something. A failed closing or a failure to even land a listing in the first place is an opportunity to look at what you've gained during the experience. One part of the equation that people often forget is the new experience and knowledge found in the process. Now that the deal is totally lost, you have to ask yourself, "What did I learn from this?" There is always something to learn from every deal, whether it closes or not. Maybe it doesn't seem like much at the time, but a little bit of experience and knowledge goes a long way. Every situation you learn from chips away at your flaws, making you a better and better agent. Do not take this lightly.

A bigger point behind this is about **attitude**. Trust me. I see listings pop up all the time that I thought I should have had. But I just brush it off and keep moving forward. You must realize that there are plenty of agents out there and your personality is not going to match up with every single client in the market. You cannot take it personally. So, here's the thing: you are going to pick up listings and buyers that other agents thought they should have gotten. It is all part of it. Understand that there are unlimited deals for you in the market and it all boils down to how much work you are willing to put into it. Accepting that reality puts you on the path to a healthy attitude. The next step on that path is to embrace the positives even within what some may call a failure.

Losing deals is no longer a negative to me. In my eyes, I see it as positive thing—well, at least as a *potential* positive. I still hate to lose them, but I understand that it is part of the process and there is nothing I can do to change that except to redirect the energy upward and forward. I aim to find the best way to look at each situation so that every deal I pursue becomes a win/win.

Another part of a lost deal that I have never heard anyone talking about is the future time that is given back to you. For example, if you missed a listing to another agent, now you don't have to spend the time you would have spent securing and servicing that listing. Nor do you have to worry about spending any more time with a prospect who doesn't want to do business with you. Therefore, you get that future time back to pursue other deals. Think about it for a minute: when you lose a deal, you have all this time back that you don't have to spend on that deal anymore, and you are a better agent with all this new experience and knowledge you just gained. You also may have just avoided a problematic deal or a mismatched client. Instead of being depressed and ruminating about it, be positive. Take the extra time and new skills and go get five more deals in the same time frame.

Another angle I take when I lose a deal is to use it as **motivation**. I re-direct my disappointment into positive energy and get fired up with a determination to get the next listing or make the next closing. I love it!

Let me add an important secret: half the deals/clients I "lose" eventually come back to me. Why? Because I handled the bad situation professionally and positively. I did what I was supposed to do on the relationship side of things.

Let's walk through an example. Say I had a listing under contract and the buyer's financing fell through. In some situations, I might work with the buyer to suggest other financing options (unless it was plainly obvious that was impossible at the time). The buyer saw my diligence and care and thus became a potential client or referral source for the future. But let's say we quickly learned there was nothing we could do to keep the deal together. I did not let the client (the seller) see any negativity, whining or disappointment in my eyes or attitude. I handled the situation pleasantly and professionally, and made sure the seller was updated at all times and let him know we will find another buyer. Chances are high that the seller will understand and allow me to keep the listing until we find another buyer.

On the flip side, if I had failed to stay in close contact with the seller, and only let him know at the last minute that the deal was falling through, he might fire me and find a different agent.

Again, the same thing applies with a buyer who goes under contract with you, and halfway through the deal finds out that she can't get the loan. If you treat this situation professionally and respectfully, the buyer will stick with you until she can qualify for a loan or finds alternative financing.

Most lost deals are not lost forever. Some are, but even then, I use every experience as a way to take my level of understanding to the next level. I absolutely do not talk or even think about deals that fell through. Do not sulk about them. Regretting and sulking about lost deals keeps you in a negative mood, plus takes time away from finding more deals to replace the one you lost. Use a *fail* to motivate you to move to the next *success*.

Just as we have limited time, we also have limited mental energy. Do not waste your mental energy on things you cannot change. Negative thoughts and attitudes will suck the life out of you emotionally, and will "take up the space" in your brain that you should instead be using to move forward. If you can use my method of losing deals with acceptance and no regret, and seek to learn and grow, and most of all, to enthusiastically go get more deals out of it, your business will dramatically improve in the coming months.

Chapter 5: Handling Buyers

If you are going to be a great listing agent and make decisions that multiply your time and provide the best opportunities for your success, you must know how to handle buyers. Picking and choosing the right buyers to work with and which ones to refer to others is a significant skill that many agents haven't honed. As a listing agent, you should only take a buyer if they meet one or more of the following criteria:

- Past Client/Sphere of Influence
- Direct Referral
- Buyer who wants to buy one of your listings
- Current Owner who wants to Buy

These are the only reasons to take a buyer if you are truly a listing agent. Taking a buyer that you get from anywhere else can distract you from achieving your listing goals. When a listing agent receives buyers from any other source other than the ones just mentioned, he or she should qualify them as a wanted buyer, or else refer them to a buyer's agent. This way no time is wasted on the buyer. Remember, if the referred buyer does in fact close a transaction through the agent you sent them to, the listing agent (you) who referred the buyer still gets a referral fee. You will get this referral fee for *zero* time invested. How efficient is that? You'd be getting paid for something that you have absolutely no time invested in.

Meanwhile, you could take that same time you may have spent with the one buyer and spread it out with dozens of potential sellers. See what happened here? The listing agent had a potential buyer that did not come from one of my "good reasons to take a buyer." The agent decided not to move forward with them, so referred them to a buyer's agent. While the buyer's agent was selling that buyer a property, the listing agent is simultaneously connecting with scores of potential clients, creating/maintaining great relationships and still getting a referral fee for doing little to nothing. It doesn't get better than that.

This is the mindset of listing agents/top producers. They multiply their time and create possibilities for many more opportunities at the same time. This is the art of real estate: putting yourself in the best situations for maximum results.

Learn to Earn

It takes time to learn and become effective with this. Experience is vital when it comes to knowing which actions to take and which to avoid. As an agent—experienced or not—who wants to produce more, you must obtain more experience and learn from your mistakes. The more experience under your belt, the better. Trust me, it never ends.

If you are looking hard enough, regardless of your experience, you will always learn something new. The market has a mind of its own and does what it wishes. Never assume that you have the market figured out. Always assume that you have no idea what the market is going to do. We are here to help people achieve their real estate goals, not to predict the market. When someone wants to buy or sell, it's our job to go above and beyond to make that happen for them.

When to Take Buyers

Let's talk about the different reasons a listing agent would take a buyer. First of all, listing agents are not *opposed* to buyers, and never *call* themselves "Listing Agents," nor would they advertise as such. This would only close the door of opportunity to helping clients *buy* properties. Remember, listing agents are top producing dealmakers. They want to do any deal they can that makes sense, timewise and financially. The difference is that they pick and choose their spots and the type of buyers they work with. Some agents may call this greedy or discriminative. But the fact is that top producers want to help as many people as they can, so time is valuable. If they have to turn one client down so that they can spend the same time helping five others, how is that greedy? They are trying to give service to more people.

If you are helping one buyer at a time, you can't possibly help hundreds. Every time you say *yes* to one client, you are essentially saying *no* to many others. Be very choosy of which clients you decide to spend time on. Experience will teach you how to handle these situations. You will not learn all of this here or in any other book. You must take action and learn from experience.

Past Clients/Sphere of Influence

A past client is obviously a client who has already completed a transaction with you. This is someone you connected with, followed up with, converted into a client and negotiated a deal with. You stayed in contact with them after the sale. They appreciate the way you handled yourself during the previous transaction and they came back to you once they decided to move forward on another transaction. This is the kind of client that you wake up in the morning for. You invested significant time with this person and built a great relationship. And now all your hard work is paying off. You have earned their trust for life. You have had lunches, helped them move furniture, called and checked on them from time to time, sent market reports, helped their friends and family. These are the things you must do to keep relationships strong.

At some point, they decide it's time to buy a property. Who do you think they are going to call? Exactly. The agent who has been there for them. The agent who works hard and is dependable. The agent who looks out for their best interest at all times. You! So, they pick up the phone or shoot you an email letting you know they are ready to buy.

You then discuss what they are looking for. It doesn't matter to you what type of property they are seeking, except to help them get what they want. Of course, you are going to help them regardless of what type of property they are seeking. At this point we are more interested in doing whatever we can in order to maintain and grow this relationship further. Remember, think quality here. Take time with this buyer and let them know that they are a high priority to you. This is a client who will always come back to you, plus they will send you plenty of great referrals. Treat them well.

Direct Referrals

A direct referral could be a buyer or a seller. In this case, we are talking about a buyer referral. If a past client, or another agent, thought enough about you and your services to send you a referral, then they deserve for you to prove them right. Honor their trust. When you receive a referral, this means that you made such a good impression on the person sending you the referral that they felt confident and comfortable enough to send you someone who could use your services. That says a lot about the level of esteem that person has for you; it's the highest compliment you could receive. From among the hundreds of other agents out there, they picked you to receive this potential buyer.

Let's say a satisfied past client, named Joe, thinks so highly of you, he refers a friend, Jane. Don't you think you should have an equal amount of esteem for Joe? Show that respect by treating Joe's friend, Jane, like she is family, regardless of the type of property she is looking for. Even if it turns out that Jane is not very serious about buying, you will still spend the time it takes to make sure Joe knows his referrals are treated as a high priority.

Whether they buy this month or two years from

now is not even the issue. It's your job to create and maintain the relationship. Period. This will send a positive message back to the person who sent you the referral, solidifying their belief that you were the right choice, thus encouraging them to continue sending you more referrals. They know you won't embarrass them by treating their friends poorly. Take care of all direct referrals and be sure to express your gratitude to the sender as well. A gift, a phone call and a hand-written "Thank You" note are great ways to do this.

Buyer for Your Listing

If you happen to get a sign call or an Internet lead from a potential buyer who is asking for more information on one of your listings, this is another great opportunity to take a buyer. You owe it to your seller to pursue any possibilities that might help sell their property. Jump all over this buyer and make sure that you follow up accordingly. They may or may not be serious, but treat them as if they are ready to buy. Make yourself readily available to them if they would like to see the property. Find any answers to questions they may have. Let them know that you are available to help them in any way possible, always just a phone call away.

Go down this path as far as you can take it. You never know where it might lead. Be diligent and honest with them. Do not try to sway them to your listing if it's not exactly what they are looking for. Make sure you are looking out for their best interests even if you are also representing the seller. This is vital for your future relationship with this buyer, plus for your broader reputation. Integrity and professionalism should overrule everything when it comes to these sticky situations. If they are willing to make an offer on your listing, that's great. Write it up and present it to the seller. Negotiate a fair deal for both parties and watch everyone walk away from the closing table smiling and praising your services. Plus, getting in on both sides of a deal isn't a bad thing either! Take these buyers as a high priority and handle them with care.

Current Owner Who wants to Buy

A seller who also wants to buy a property is my favorite type of buyer. Whether they are upgrading or downgrading, or just want to add another property to their portfolio, either way, this is a great situation to be in as the agent. Here you are concentrating on listings and out of nowhere, one of your possible sellers tells you they would like to buy. Perfect! This is the highest quality "buyer lead" known to real estate. They know what they want and how to get it. Already owning property, they know the ins and outs of ownership. Therefore, you don't have to educate them from square one—saving you time.

With such a buyer, spend as much time as you need to make them feel like they are your Number One client. Researching, meeting, showing and following up with them all become a high priority.

This is your opportunity to prove to them how great of a buyer's agent you can be. By doing this, you give them a very high amount of confidence that you are the best *listing* agent for them when they decide to sell. Even if you feel like they aren't that serious about buying, get them the information they asked about and follow up with them promptly. Make sure that they know that if they list their property with you later, you will do the same with any potential buyer who might inquire.

This is a powerful technique that will grow your business by leaps and bounds. Having this long-term career outlook and making decisions accordingly will put you in position to help thousands of people, and of course it will provide you with a great income. Short-term decisions, such as advertising for buyers or wasting too much time with every buyer that comes along, will not.

Be Resilient

A listing agent doesn't shrink at the thought of rejection, nor crumble even when actually rejected. We embrace it. Listing agents know that rejection is going to happen over 80% of the time. However, they also know that without enduring the 80% rejection rate, they would never reap the rewards of the 20% acceptance. You cannot have one without the other. If you look at a list of a top producer's closed transactions, it only represents a small percentage of the transactions they *actually* pursued.

An outside observer doesn't see the other transactions that had been pursued *unsuccessfully*. From the outside, people only see the successes not the failures. This creates a mirage for other agents. Other agents may think that high producers have a Midas Touch, only getting the deals that work out and the prospects who buy and sell the first time they meet. The truth is that top producing agents do not turn everything they touch into gold. They started out the same way every agent starts out, with nothing. No deals, no clients, no direction. And even as they begin having some success, they will still have "failures" (but weren't really failures because they may have yielded connections and relationships that later paid off).

If we all start out the same way, then why do some agents make it and most do not? It's because top producers have **resilience**. They have resilience when it comes to everything: resilient to rejection, never giving up, working hard, learning, sticking with relationships, seeking self-development, relentless in reaching goals… everything. Most agents, and people in general, do not have the resilience it takes to succeed. Do you? Ask yourself: "Do I have the resilience to succeed in this business? Will I allow anything to get in my way? Will I make excuses if I don't succeed? Will I start making phone calls and collecting email addresses today? Do I want this bad enough to sacrifice my lifestyle?" Success is a lifestyle. You must live the lifestyle of a top producer and understand the principals that they live by. Wake up every day with a routine and mission to accomplish your goals. Be resilient.

Be a buyer's agent only for the right reasons and watch your time start multiplying right before your eyes. Suddenly you have more deals and more time to pursue business instead of chasing your tail all the time. The difference maker for you will be if you take this information and use it. Put it to work. See for yourself what works and does not work. Then take those experiences and create more business, making better decisions, growing each step of the way. Most agents know what they should be doing and how to do it. They have heard it time and time again. But they never act. They spend all their time on getting ready to get started.

Forget everything about "getting ready." If you don't have a client ready to buy or sell a property, then what do you have to get ready for? Start making contacts today, right now. Find people, make connections and start helping them achieve their goals. Figure out all the other stuff later.

Chapter 6: The Power of Compounding Efforts

Have you ever asked yourself how certain people got to the level of success they are at? Sit back and consider agents who have hit Diamond ($1,000,000 in gross commissions within one year); it's amazing what it took to get there. Once you are there, however, it seems like it happened in the blink of an eye. But when one considers the *gross* sales the Diamond level represents, the efforts seem like massive, almost-impossible feats! The truth is that what made it possible was **compounding** efforts. Over time your consistent actions start to snowball into massive results that continue growing and growing because you pushed it uphill so long until finally it starts rolling downhill.

Indeed, think of your business as a snowball. In the beginning, it's just a few "flakes" —very small, almost non-existent. It is your job to combine the random flakes into a tiny snowball and start pushing it up the hill, adding more and more snowflakes to it. As you push, you gain momentum and it starts to grow. The more you push it, the bigger it gets and the faster it grows. Over time, you'll get past the uphill climb (as in, beyond the initial "learning curve,"), and things roll more easily. If you keep pushing long and hard enough, your snowball grows into a huge boulder of a snowball that has enormous downhill momentum. Before long you have a large enough snowball, with gravity and moment on your side, to sustain a long and prosperous career. But you can never stop rolling and never stop growing the size of your snowball. You must always add snowflakes, or new business, or it will shrink and melt. Once it melts, all of your efforts are lost and you have to start all over again.

I see many agents who work hard and gain lots of momentum, only to take a few weeks or months off. When they finally come back to work, they are starting over from the bottom of the hill again. They struggle to regain momentum. Once they get it going again, they take more time off, until they eventually get tired of the roller coaster of ups and downs. There are some very talented agents who could sell the pants off of me out there, but because I am willing to outwork them for the rest of my life, I win. I produce fives times as much as other agents who could and should be outselling me—simply because I want it more and I am willing to put the work in. And because I understand compounding and momentum: the snowball effect.

Let's try a different metaphor: an airplane. In the beginning of your career, or at any point in your career that you want to double and triple your current business, it's like a plane at takeoff. When the plane starts down the runway, it burns an enormous amount of fuel and energy to get off the ground. Then, once in midair, it continues to burn fuel to climb to the desired altitude. Once the plane reaches the desired altitude, the pilot can ease back on the throttle. This is called the cruising altitude. Thanks to aerodynamic engineering, at cruising altitude the plane moves forward with ease and can go great distances and speeds with relatively little fuel.

Think of your business the same way. When you first start, you need to burn lots of fuel and energy to get off the ground. In the beginning of my career, that required working 14-hour days. Once you are midair, you must continue burning tons of energy and fuel to continue to the desired altitude. The distance between taking off and cruising altitude is going to be far more than you can imagine. However, if you can keep pushing long and hard enough, you can reach cruising altitude. Once you reach it, it is your job as the pilot to keep the plane on track. You can't fall asleep at the wheel, or have any distractions. Just as with a pilot, you must remain keenly focused and continue on the course you have set.

When I first started in real estate in 2002, I was just 20 years old. I guessed (correctly) that to overcome the handicap of being so young, I would need to work harder than normal. So I spent all of my time making cold calls—and lots of them. I would call fifty prospects a day. Every night I would look up 100 phone numbers using a reverse address lookup website. I could only find about half of them. Then half of those were bad numbers. I would end up leaving about 20 voicemails and talking to about 5 people. And this was long before today's world of dialing systems that can find a number, dial it, and leave a message for you. It is an amazing time in history for real estate agents who know the path to success and overlook all the garbage training information out there.

Anyway, other agents were looking at me like I was crazy. I would work all night looking up prospects' home phone numbers (which most people don't even have anymore), just to talk to 5 people on average. They thought I was nuts. It seemed like far too much work just to talk to a few people. But what they didn't realize was that I was targeting certain property owners who owned prime property, connecting with two or three a day. And, I was connecting with them on such a meaningful level that I knew most of them would choose me as their agent when the time came.

I did this every single day for two years while other agents laughed, saying what I was doing would never work. Two or three connections a day got me ten a week, forty a month, 500 in a year and over 1,000 in two years. It's the compounding that takes you to that higher level that no one can figure out how to get to.

The small amount of quality work I did added up to yield an incredible result over time. Once I completed that feat, no one understood how I had accomplished it. These were the same agents who doubted me. They watched exactly what I was doing, but still could not believe that it got me where I was. They thought I must have been doing something else that they did not know about. Wrong! There was no magic secret. It's just making the small extra effort every day— relentlessly— that adds up. That's how you build a big business.

Over the course of those two years, I connected with a thousand Gulf-front condo owners and closed over thirty transactions. When I say, "a thousand," that's not a figure of speech for "a bunch." I mean literally, actually 1,000! Out of that number, thirty transactions may not seem like much. But the more important point is that the scores of relationships I created during that time continued over the years, bringing many more deals since.

As of the time of writing this book, I have closed over **one hundred deals each year for the last three years** and just had my best month. As busy as I am, I still find time to make at least 50 cold calls a week. I do this because I understand the power of compounding my efforts and the importance of cold calling in growing my business. I never want my snowball to melt, and I want my business to continue to grow.

As a single agent, there's a real limit to how many deals a person can make in a year's time. So now my strategy moving forward is to work towards a higher price-per-transaction average. The way I am doing this is by targeting my 50 calls per week, calling mostly those who own property worth one million dollars and up. This will, over time, increase my price-per-transaction results.

If you notice, even though I am at an already high level of success, I am still looking for ways to get better. This is a true mark of a top producer. Every day, I wake up and search for a way to get better and take my life to the next level. There is no such thing as being at "the Top," there is always another step to take. The Top is a fairytale. It's a made-up place that doesn't exist. Every day to me is exactly like my first day in the business. I am hungry to learn and produce. I start each day at zero and try to take it to one hundred… not to reach "the Top," but to reach my personal best and full potential.

Compound your efforts each day and slowly build your business to the level you wish and plan for. Nothing happens overnight. When I used to make those calls every day, knowing that I wouldn't get much immediate fruit, that was hard at times. But I knew that the long-term effects would bear fruit. Map out your career and start planting the seeds for a great harvest.

Chapter 7: Are Cold Calls a Thing of The Past?

This chapter is adapted from a blog post I wrote about the relevance of cold calls in today's tech-based world. If you want to visit my blog, the address is www.zerotodiamond.com/blog.

In today's technology-based world full of social media and public real estate websites, most agents believe cold calling is a thing of the past. Is it? Maybe it is. Agents can communicate with far more people at lightning speed these days. You can post on Facebook, create a Tweet or email thousands of people in a blink of an eye, sending any information you want for free. It could be general market information, a direct offer to buy or sell a property or just checking in on a personal level. Consider how far the world has come in terms of communication technology in recent years. Amazing! Millennials wake up in the morning and spend 15-30 minutes on their phones, scrolling through their social media of choice before they even climb out of bed. All ages use some form of "hi-tech" communicaton device(s).

The world is changing at a more rapid pace than ever before. And the world of real estate is no different. Today's buyers are far more electronically connected than they were 5-10 years ago— and thus much more educated. They know what properties they want to be shown before they even talk to their agent, which makes the agent's job easier. The buyer also knows what has sold and when it closed. They often do all their research online and already know which property they want, and likely have studied comparable properties and prices. They know what they want to offer, and what price they think they will end up negotiating. They have studied the sales-price to listing-price ratios of comparable properties and understand the market more thoroughly than buyers did a decade ago. And they are becoming more educated as we speak.

Since the beginning of the real estate industry, personal contact via cold calling was the fastest way to a high level of success. Is this still true today? Well, one thing has definitely not changed over the years: *conversation*. The one thing between any real estate agent and a closing is a conversation. Think about it. How many transactions happen without a single conversation? Few, if any. The common denominator for most all closings is that a conversation was had between the agent and the prospective buyer or seller. Even if the prospect is an internet lead or came from some sort of social media platform, there then had to be a conversation solidifying the deal.

This is what makes real estate so unique. Technology has not been able to replace real estate agents the same way it has replaced people in so many other occupations. Why is this? It is because real estate is so **local**. If someone wants to buy property in your area, even if the buyer is from Timbuktu and found the property using the internet, they will most likely still want and need a local realtor. You! And why wouldn't they? In most markets, real estate services for buyers is free of charge. Every local market is so entirely different and ever-changing that people need a local expert to help them navigate through any transaction.

Since the market needs local experts to help customers navigate the marketplace and there is no way that technology can replace this need, real estate agents are still thriving in this new, high-tech world. If anything, technology has helped the local realtor more than hurting us. The software systems get easier to use with each passing year. But whether technology is used or not used in any particular property search and purchase, local agents and a conversation is still needed.

The customers want a conversation with an informed, intelligent realtor who can help them understand the market. There's a lot of money involved. If a home purchase moves forward, it is a very personal, important thing. So they are not going to buy it on Amazon or at the dollar store or from a robot! A conversation with a local agent cannot be replaced with anything else. If we could replace the conversation with some form of technology, then we wouldn't need real estate agents anymore. As long as real estate has the huge human element, your job is safe.

Legalzoom.com didn't destroy the need for "human lawyers." WebMD did not bankrupt your local doctor. Fidelity.com and eTrade didn't take out stock brokers. You can buy a car online via various sites and methods, but look around. Do you see any shortage of used car lots and new car dealers? The desire for personal and local professionals is especially true when it comes to our homes. If I need a plumbing repair, I will definitely be calling a professional. This is true in real estate as well. Forsalebyowner.com didn't take us out, and Zillow's instant offers is no threat. Sure, a small percentage of the public is willing and savvy enough to try to sell their property by owner. The vast majority give up and end up contacting a realtor in the end. Most people do not want to deal with showings, contracts, negotiations, lenders, inspectors, appraisers, title companies, lawyers, buyers, and the vaious risks involved in "do-it-yourself" selling. Therefore, **there will always be a market for agents.**

So, if the world still needs real estate agents because we need to speak to them about the local market trends, and the common denominator between all agents and their next closing is a conversation, then wouldn't the best strategy to help agents complete more transactions per year be to **have as many conversations as humanly possible?** The answer is obviously YES. Cold calling is king for the very reason why technology has not replaced real estate agents.

I have built my entire career over the phone. In my opinion, there is no other way to build a really huge business in real estate. I have been preaching this forever while actually proving it with results. Every agent I tell this too always thinks they can build a huge business a different way. They try everything they can do to avoid making phone calls. If they would just put a fraction of the energy they used to avoid cold calling into just making the calls, they would be so far ahead. They all try, and they all have fallen short as far as I have seen. Sure, I have seen some agents do well with other methods, but I haven't seen anyone firsthand build a $1,000,000 a year business while neglecting phone calls. What gets me is that here I am as living proof, yet as motivated as some agents claim to be, they just won't listen to me. They argue that they have a better way. Trust me, I have tried many other ways.

You build your business over the phone, and you build your name brand with everything else. Everything else means *everything else*: websites, signs, billboards, bench ads, postcards, emails, letters, social media, etc. There's nothing wrong with having those things. But they are of little value without phone calling. Consider your phone as your best friend and partner in realty.

Chapter 8: The Magic Questions

In this chapter, I am going to lay out a basic roadmap of questions that you can use with any prospect, any buyer or seller, to take them to the exact place that you want them as a valued client in your database. The goal is to go down the same road with every prospect and try to end up in the same place. But of course, every road has forks. The trick is to know what to do when you come to a fork in the road to maximize the results to your advantage. So let's get into it. This is one of my favorite subject matters to discuss.

Whether you are working with a buyer or a seller, it's the same map either way. Step one is to determine if they want to proceed with a deal or not. You may ask them if they have considered selling lately. In which case, they could say *Yes* or *No*. Maybe they called you and said they are thinking of selling. This could mean that they are ready to sell. Or a buyer calls you about buying a house. Or you called them offering them one of your listings that they might be interested in. Whatever the scenario, the point is that either your prospect is ready to move forward with a deal, or they are not. This is the first fork in the road.

Left Fork: Not Interested?

Let's first talk about the fork to the left: let's say that they tell you they are **not** interested in buying or selling at this time. Once you establish that they are not interested, the very next question to them should be, "I understand… well, let me ask you: is there another agent in the area you might work with if you *were* ready?" This is a critical question. If they reply that they do have an ongoing relationship with another agent in the area, then it's time to move on. Regardless of how much they might end up liking you, chances are they will not use you if their mom, brother, uncle or best friend from high school is an agent. That is not to say that they will never switch agents. That happens all the time and is part of the business. The point is that there is no need to try to force it at this time.

Although you are "moving on" from this prospect, you are not abandoning them. You can adapt/use the script (magic question) in the next paragraph to obtain their contact info, so they can still get mail from you, if you wish. At the least, they will still see your signs all over town and may see you talking/posting about the local real estate market on social media. Over time, they will see your success and may decide to make a change later down the road. But for now, it's not worth chasing. If they answered that they have an agent in mind for when they decide to do something, ask them what the agent's name is. Then tell them, "I know that agent… you are in good hands. If there is ever anything I can do for you, please let me know. Have a good day." Now move on to the next call. We can't waste any more time on someone not ready to buy or sell and who says they have their own agent. Remember: pick and choose where you expend your valuable time.

Right Fork: Interested!

With all that said, let's get to the key question. When any prospect shows an openness to connect—which means a willingness to share their contact information with you—that is where the *magic* can happen. At any point in the conversation when you see the time is right, you simply say, "Okay. Well, one day you are going to buy or sell, and I would just like the opportunity to help you when that day comes. Would it be okay if I stayed in touch with you?" After you say this, pause for a moment and give them a chance to answer that (hopefully) it is okay if you stay in touch with them. Asking that exact question after the last statement, and then pausing, is very critical. It's critical because once they answer "Yes," you then say, "Okay, great! What's your email address?"

The order and exact wording is vital here. Asking their permission to stay in touch feels non-invasive. Most people will be more than fine with giving you permission to stay in touch. Once you get them to commit to that, then you drop the hammer, asking for their email address. It would have been harder to get their email address right up front on the first call because an email address is very personal. But because you had them commit to staying in touch *before* asking them for it, they almost feel obligated to give it to you. And you are not going to share their email with anyone or abuse it, so there is nothing unethical in asking for it.

If they refuse to give it to you, you can even ask for it again—after a bit of explanation. Tell them that it's not what they think: you will keep it private and you're not going to share it or spam them or anything like that. You just want the opportunity to stay in touch with them as the market changes moving forward.

Once you write their email address down, ask them when they might have a day soon to meet you for lunch. You want to get them to lunch to put a face with the name and get to know each other a little bit. Set the lunch appointment and go hang out with your future client.

Do you see what happened here? In this scenario, we took the left fork in the road in which the prospect tells us that they are not interested in buying or selling anything in the near future. We then took that NO, and transformed it into a lifelong relationship. We established that they do not have a current relationship in place with another agent, we got their email address and took them to lunch. This is how it's done. If you can make phone calls all day, looking for them to say they aren't interested and turn that into a lunch appointment, you will build a huge business.

Now let's continue walking with our prospect down the fork in the road to the right. In this scenario, the prospect has told us that they are possibly interested in buying or selling. Once you establish that they are interested in possibly doing something, find out more information about the situation. Finding out why a client wants to buy or sell is the real secret behind helping them accomplish their goals.

When someone decides to buy or sell a piece of property, something is going on in their *life* that is prompting them to do this. Did they get a new job or lose a job? Did their housing needs (or tastes or desires) change? Did their kids go to college? Did someone die or was someone born? Is this just strictly an investment decision? Something is happening in their life that is causing this possible transaction. Of course, you don't want to pry into their personal lives in an intrusive way. Let them talk. Listen. Let the information come organically with as little prodding from you as possible.

Until you fully understand the situation that they are in, you can't really help them the way you need to. Why do they want to buy or sell? This is the question you must find an answer to. You will sense when it's the right time to ask this question. And you will fit it into the conversation where it does not seem like an interrogation. In some situations, you may need to set the stage by saying something like, "The more I know about what you want to do, what your goals are, the more I can help you. So…." In other cases, if you will just be patient and listen, they will volunteer the answers without a question even being asked.

Once you find out that they are ready to move forward *and* you know the motives behind their decision, then you can help them accomplish their goals to the highest level. Helping them reach the highest level of satisfaction is our number one priority.

Hopefully this helps you understand where to take conversations you have with prospects under any situation. This road map can be followed in most any scenario to your advantage to build lifelong relationships with hundreds of future clients. That is the key to high production. A full Circle Prospecting Road Map can be found on www.zerotodiamond.com. Now let's go get some listings!

Chapter 9: Where to Find Listings

Listings are everywhere. There are new leads for listings every day in every market. Most of them are right there in plain sight. Lots of agents don't even notice them. Once you realize where to look and how to approach them, the rest is easy. In this chapter you will learn where all the listings are—but this will be worthless information unless you promise me that you will take this information and use it! I want you to get out there and work your fingers to the bone going after listings. Never stop. Accomplish your goals and keep going.

Listen: there are only two directions you can go in life. You are either getting better, or you are getting worse. There is no such thing as maintaining. In the animal kingdom, other than winter hibernation, if you see an animal that is sitting still for more than half a day, that animal is either sick or dying. Animals know that to survive, they have to eat—and to find food, they have to move around. If you wish to find business (your "food"), you have to move! If you decide to slow down, maintain and stop learning, you are going backwards. Do something every day to get better and learn. This applies in both real estate and in life. Be the best you that you can be every moment you have. Be active.

So what you must do now is act. But how? What is the first step? And the next step after that? That's what I am here for. The rest of this book will teach you exactly how I built my business. Understand that the ideas I share with you came from the successes and failures of many agents. These techniques and philosophies, if properly acted on, will produce a prosperous career for you.

Okay, let's get started. When contacting potential sellers, the goal is *to find out if there is a connection between you and them.* You are not trying to "get the listing." Although getting the listing is the ultimate goal, this is not the approach you should take in step one. Let me explain.

Most agents have it in their mind that they must "get the listing." They ask for the listing before they even find out if they have a connection with the possible seller. When an agent asks for the listing too early, the prospect is turned off, and nine times out of ten does not do business with that agent, now or in the future. The first rule of getting listings is to earn the prospects *trust* first, and ask for the business later. Building trust involves connecting with them in a meaningful way and showing them that you are an expert in your field by supplying market information and being professional. Finding if there is a connection is the first step in gaining trust. This is where the whole process begins or ends. If there is no connection, there is little reason to continue any further.

Being pushy destroys trust. Lots of agents approach potential sellers asking for the listing right off the bat, or by saying "I have a buyer for your property." Too many agents are using these techniques. Most of the potential clients you talk to have heard it all before. They are not stupid; they can sniff out insincerity and high-pressure techniques. They are not interested in those types of approaches. Most people in general don't want to feel like they are being "sold." They can smell a desperate salesperson a mile away, and will avoid someone who is only interested in a quick sale. Don't be a salesperson. Be an agent who wants to get to know the client, help them with all their needs and who will become their realtor for life.

Enter the relationship with a message that you are not there for the sale and that you want to *help* them. You will not connect with every prospect. A number of "failures to launch" is to be expected, and absolutely okay. Remember, on average, you will get five No's before you get a YES. Embrace the No's, knowing that you only need four more before you find a YES. I learned from my first broker that a No just means "not right now." So, stay in touch with the people who told you No. It doesn't mean that they don't want to do business with you, they just don't want to do business with you *right now*. My scripts show you how to take a No and turn it into a life-long relationship, as seen in the previous chapter. I am waiting on them to tell me that they aren't interested. It gives me an opportunity to build a relationship with that prospect. Using this method, it doesn't matter if they say YES or No… either way, you win.

The day will come when you realize how much money you make by being rejected, then transitioning that rejection into a relationship for future business.

Another reason **not** to approach these prospects by asking for a listing or telling them you have a buyer is because they might be more of a buyer than a seller. You are more likely to get their business if you listen first, then understand their primary motivation, and after that, demonstrate that you are ready to address their need. Learn how to connect with your prospects, find out more about their true real estate motives and goals, and then truly help them—rather just routinely listing their property. This is not rocket science.

How do you find ways to connect with them on a much higher level than the average agent? Simple: ask questions and listen. For example, "How long have you owned the property?" The specific question doesn't matter as much as the fact that you are inviting them to talk to you, and then you are making it clear you are listening, understanding and caring. You will be surprised how much you can help a prospect once you know more about their situation. By asking questions, you show a high level of interest in their wellbeing and thus begin a strong relationship. Strong relationships equal a strong real estate business.

FSBO's & Expired Listings

For Sale By Owners (FSBO's) and Expired /Withdrawn Listings (EWL's) are normally hot leads—owners who are ready to sell in the current market, which is a good thing. However, these types of leads are only good for brand new agents to get some much-needed experience. This is not where the real money is in real estate, believe it or not. The real money is in Circle Prospecting, which we will get into in the next section. But for now, I want to get my point across to you about FSBO's and EWL's.

I feel very strongly that new agents need to call every FSBO and EWL in their area in the first week of their career. This is the #1 way to get the most amount of experience in the least amount of time. You get to talk to a live prospect who has an interest in selling, you have a good chance to set an appointment and meet a seller face-to-face, you get to view the property and have a conversation with the seller, and maybe you get the listing and thus experience the process of actually listing a property.

Maybe the seller wants to buy a property and you get to go through the process of showing properties. There are all kinds of positive experiences in pursuing FSBO's and EWL's. Remember, I have phone scripts for these on my website. In a moment, we will look at some other ways to get listings that can bring you more "income per hour" (see "circle prospecting," below). But calling FSBO's and EWL's can make you money and, as I said, provide valuable experience early in a realty career. I have even pursued this avenue at one point in my career and obtained listings that I did sell. I am not saying that this is not a profitable area of real estate. Every agent is good at something different. If you are good at FSBO's and EWL's and you feel like that is going to get you where you want to be, then go for it. I support you.

Before we leave the topic of FSBO's and EWL's, here's why you don't want to view them as the path to the top of your market. When you encounter most of these prospects, it is a high-pressure situation even before you open your mouth. They have already heard from so many agents that they have their guard up. They view you as just another agent who is trying to get their listing. Therefore, if you want to get the listing in this scenario, you may feel forced to be high pressure (which I feel is not the best way to create a lifelong relationship). Even if you have a shot at building a lifelong relationship with the seller, their guard is up too high at that moment; they are resistant to all agents (so don't take it personally).

I'm not trying to discourage you—just giving you lowered expectations and caution. You can still connect with some of them if you find the right approach and the balance between patience and persistence. All sellers will not be the same and you may end up with some lifelong clients out of the experience, so again, I urge all new agents to eagerly go after FSBO's and EWL's full force until the needed amount of experience is found. After you get your feet wet and get some experience under your belt, it is time to move on to where the real money is.

Circle Prospecting (Farming)

Circle Prospecting is **targeting a group** of owners who own property that you would like to sell by cold calling, sending direct mail, digitally advertising, etc. When you target a niche market and communicate with the owners in the proper manner, you will see your listing inventory increase dramatically. What group of owners do we target? Well, that is up to you. You must decide what specific type(s) of property you would like to sell and become an expert about.

Every agent needs an area in the market in which they feel comfortable enough to consider themselves an expert. Maybe you picked up a few FSBO's and EWL's and liked the type of property involved, so you decided to start targeting that group of owners in the same subdivision, condominium or road. Or, maybe you want to sell houses or condos priced between $300,000-$500,000. Selecting a group of owners that fit together and communicating with the group on a regular basis is called *farming*. Farming is a must for all agents. Constant communication with past, current and future clients will be the backbone of your overall success. But, of course, you have limited time and money and resources, so you are not going to target the entire United States. Most farmers have a set amount of acreage in a proscribed area and don't try to farm in five different counties (unless they hire additional farm hands, of course). This is why we call it farming: you select your "North Forty" and you work that ground, planting and nurturing until harvest!

When selecting what type of property you will become a specialist of, and a group of owners in that niche to start with, you must find what I like to call the *"sweet spot"* in the market. The sweet spot in your market is the highest price range properties that are turning over the quickest. In other words, what type of property in your market has the best balance of transactions versus price? You can research this on your local MLS. Pull up all the closed sales in your area for the last year and start studying. Look for a type of property (or subdivision/complex) that sells very often. Maybe it's single-family homes between $150,000-$250,000. Maybe it's condos between $200,000-$300,000. Maybe it's land and lots. You have to do the research and decide what type of property you feel good about. Make your decision based on the long term as you will begin to build your brand around being a specialist of this type of property.

Once you decide on the type of property and group of specific properties you want to target, it is time to go to whatever system your broker uses to find the owners' names and addresses, or this can be found in county records. Figure out the best way to find the information and put them into your database.

Adopt a system that will help you keep track of your farming efforts. Once you have picked out the group of owners you want to farm, the best formula begins with a letter. After that, send a postcard every month… forever. Every now and then, if you have new information or an interesting point you would like to get across to them, send another letter. These frequent mailouts are the foundation for future relationships with the owners in your farm group.

Farming can bring you immediate business and long-term business. It will bring you plenty of great relationships that turn into clients and referrals. Once you have sent the first letter out, go ahead and collect as many phone numbers as you can from this group and get ready to call them. A week after the letter was sent, follow up with a phone call. When you **add a follow-up phone call** to the mail-outs, that alone increases your success rate over just doing mailouts by over 600%. Would you like to increase your success rate by 600%? I sure hope so.

This business is hard enough. If there is a way you can increase your success rate by 600%, you'd better take advantage of it. Generally, mailouts alone will create only a 3% success rate (that is, with no follow-up phone call). And doing mail alone would take much longer to bear fruit, because on average it takes seven pieces of mail in the prospects hands before they even recognize your name! When you add the follow-up phone call into the equation, your success rate not only jumps up to 18%, but it also happens much faster. Take advantage of this information, please!

Call them up, ask them if they got your letter and if they have considered buying or selling lately. If they say *No*, use the Magic Questions (Chapter 8) to get the email address and create the relationship. Make sure they know you are always here for them if there is anything they may need, and that you will always stay in touch with them. Try for a lunch appointment. Having lunch with as many property owners (whether or not ready to buy or sell right now) as you can is a huge tactic of mine and has paid dividends over the years.

Once you have called all the owners who got one

of your letters, pick out another group of owners to start calling without the initial letter, and keep calling. The most important activity you can do to create business is to call property owners. And the good thing is that you could never call all of them. Once you understand that, you realize that you can make as much money as you want depending on how much you want to work. Use my ZTD Circle Prospecting Phone Script for these owners and start collecting email addresses. Think of yourself as a full-time email collector and information provider, and a part-time real estate agent.

We are going to take these email addresses and send a weekly market report that keep the long-term relationship in place forever. To see an example, start receiving my weekly reports for free just by testing LISTTOLAST to 22828.

I used to call 100 numbers per day as a new agent. I suggest you do the same, or more, if you want your goals to match your results. If you took this one path and mastered it, you have a strong possibility of becoming the highest producer in your area. This is the exact path that took me to the top of my market.

Become great at talking on the phone and having a conversation. Connect with people not as a sales agent, but as a new friend who only wants to see them succeed. This will draw them toward you and give you a great start to possibly becoming their agent when the time is right.

To recap: send mail every month to your farm group, follow-up with phone calls, build relationships, help buyers and sellers with transactions, have closings, get referrals, stay in touch with past, present and future clients, and have fun being an agent.

This business can be exciting, enjoyable and rewarding. Each person you help should involve an enjoyable experience for everyone. Cherish the fact that you are able to sell real estate and don't take it for granted.

Sphere of Influence/Past Clients

These prospects either already know you personally, or have done business with you in the past. Both are, by definition, someone you need to stay in touch with and ask for business and seek referrals from. Talk with them frequently and make sure you are up-to-date with all their real estate goals. Make sure they know you are available 24/7 for anything they may need.

Sometimes agents don't let everyone they know that they are in real estate. Make sure *all* your friends and family know that you are in the business and are ready to serve them if they could use your services. Don't be a pest, but do find ways to remind friends and family that you are actively seeking to help people with their real estate needs. That's easy with Facebook friends and family. It may require more thought, creativity and activity to find ways to keep other friends and family reminded… again, without being pushy.

Past clients have already experienced your service,

and after a great experience, should choose you to be their agent in the future. This group should always be asked if they know of anyone who may be interested in buying or selling in the near future. Referrals are king with this group. Past clients may also include clients from some form of non-realty business you were involved in before becoming a realtor. If those clients (or colleagues/workmates) had a good experience with you and know you to be hardworking, honorable and trustworthy in your previous endeavor, they will likely also trust you in your new business of real estate.

Business Now and Later

While you are making prospecting calls to obtain listings, you will run into people who are looking to buy or sell a property in the very near future. This is immediate business. Follow up with these prospects in an urgent manner and ride these situations out until you make a sale or hit a brick wall. Some will turn into sales and some will not. That's part of the game. But through your efforts of concentrating on listings and creating relationships, you will end up with both immediate and long-term business. Wouldn't that be great?

Now you have a roadmap, a direction you can follow that will yield business today and tomorrow. The sky is the limit. Make prospecting calls all day every day until you are so busy that you need an assistant. By the time you are that busy, you will be able to afford one!

Chapter 10: The Listing Appointment

Now that you know what you should be doing all day (calling property owners) and you have some direction, you will start running into owners who have contemplated selling their property and would like to know how much it is worth. This may lead to a listing, or it may not. Once you find the market value of the property, that price may not be enough to make the seller move forward, which is fine. The goal is not to pressure them, so that later, when they do sell the property, you will be their agent.

Rule number one in pricing properties is to never price a property without doing a walkthrough. Therefore, it's ShowTime! Time to dress appropriately and put on your business face to meet the owner. When you show up to the appointment, it's good to be exactly on time. Knock on the door at the exact time that you agreed to. This will show that you are prompt and can be trusted to do what you say you will do, *when* you said you will do it. This is very important when it comes to first impressions.

First, bring with you a folder. Order professional-looking folders printed with your company logo, with flaps on the inside that will hold your business cards. Inside the folder, include all the market information that is important to the subject property, including recent closed sales and active/pending listings. Have these in a table format on one sheet of paper, not one property per page. This makes the information easy to examine.

Second, have all the listing documents ready to fill out and get signed. Just leave this blank until you get confirmation that the owner is ready to list the property with you.

Third, have a one sheet resume or bio on yourself. You can include whatever information you wish. My resume includes my professional, personal and educational history, plus a few testimonials or endorsement quotes from happy clients.

The last thing I include in the folder is a gift card from a nice restaurant in the area. I normally do $15-20, but you can do $10 if you wish. Anything you give them at this point will set you apart from the average agent.

Another thing that I bring with me is a personalized pen. I have a few hundred pens made every quarter, inscribed with my name, company and phone number. So I show up with my professional-looking folder full of great info, plus a gift card and a personalized pen. At the end of the meeting, regardless if we signed papers or not, I hand them the entire folder to keep.

Appearances Matter

It is said, "Don't judge a book by its cover." But let's be honest: within moments, most people make an initial assessment of you and your professionalism (or lack of it). When I show up, dressed professionally with my folder in hand, I introduce myself and shake their hand. I display professionalism along with a genuine smile. I do not overdress—wearing a suit, for example, would only look fake in my market. Be authentic.

Only after they ask me to come in will I set a foot inside their doorway. Once they open the door wide and gesture or invite me in, I walk in and wait for them to direct us to sit down, or, as often happens, they first give me a tour of the property. Normally, I put my folder on a table or counter as they start to show me their home. I allow them to take control and walk me through the place telling me every little detail about their home or other property. Most of the time, the owner will be trying to tell me why their property is worth more than everybody else's. **At this point, I certainly do not argue price even if their expectations seem unrealistic.** I listen to everything they say, showing genuine interest. At this stage, you play along with them and make them feel very comfortable with you. This is not being fake, its simply being polite and open. Who knows? They may convince me that there are real reasons why their property IS worth more than similar properties.

When they get through showing you their property and telling you everything about it, you may get caught in a conversation that is non-real estate related. Go with the flow and use this opportunity to build the relationship. At the right point, it will come time to talk shop. This is when you sit down with them wherever you had placed your folder, open it up and pull out the comparable sales/active listings out. Show it to them and look through the information together, comparing their property to the comparable properties that have sold. After they have seen the numbers, you can be more realistic with them about the listing price and see how they react. You never know how someone will react to reality, but it's your job to be realistic with them in the end.

Once you have showed them the information, it is up to them to make the decision from there. Do they want to list it? Do they want to list it with you? What price do they want to ask? Etc. Allow them to make all the decisions. You are only there to provide them with the detailed market information. Remember, low-pressure is key. Do not try to force them to sell or list with you. This will create a negative experience for them and they will never contact you again. Our goal is not a quick, forced "close," but rather a long-term relationship with years of business and referrals.

If you feel like they want to list the property, but aren't being decisive with you about it, it is okay to tell them that you feel like they should go ahead and put it on the market. Then sit back and see how they react. If they do decide to list with you, immediately start filling out the paperwork. If they ultimately decide not to list with you right now, that's okay. You tell them that you will stay in close touch with them and that they can have the folder. Explain what is in the folder before you leave, if you haven't already.

This is the opposite of a high-pressure sales pitch. Trust me, agents who try that approach don't make it very far. Be prepared and confident, but lead with listening. Every listing appointment that you walk into, have the expectation that you are going to walk away with a client for life. You may not get the listing today, but over time you will show the owner that you are one of the hardest working, most honest and dependable agents in the area. That's what kind of agent an owner wants, not someone who tries to sell them on something they have no interest in. Concentrate on helping them achieve their goals first... and the deals will follow.

Chapter 11: The *Forever Follow-up* Method

A broker once told me that this business is all in the follow-up. I took that to heart, and it has proved true. If you have interested leads that you have not followed-up on, then you are not ready to start calling new prospects. **Current leads need your immediate attention. "Following-up" needs your immediate attention.** Both are necessary. The trick is to balance your prospecting time between following-up and reaching for new ones. It's like tennis. Tennis pro's will teach you that how you strike the ball (the ball's placement on the racket head, how you grip the racket, initial swing, etc.) is critical. Then the pro will also tell you that "follow-through" (how your swing continues to guide the ball) is critical. Both are key.

In Chapter 3, I discussed how lead conversion is a myth, that you should instead spend most of your time prospecting for new leads. But I also warned not to abandon follow-up—just don't allow it to take over your entire focus. Know when you are wasting your time on prospects.

Balance

Some days I alternate every call between a new prospect and a follow-up call. Other days I purely concentrate on new business, and some days I focus only on follow-up. However you choose to do that is fine, as long as there is **balance**. How well you balance these two actions will have much to do with the level of success you achieve. Low-producing agents obtain a bit of business and then start shying away from hunting new business. This is a dangerous place where you feel busy and are making money, but your business is not growing.

Remember, being an effective Listing Agent is a mindset. Listing Agents think differently than other agents. The main difference is how they make decisions about their time and energy. They are aware that they must follow-up with prospects they have started the process with, *and* that they must create interest from new prospects daily. So, as they are following up with hot leads, they are also watching the clock and calendar with new clients in mind. They won't let the day slip by without mailing or calling new leads.

Once you have made contact and feel a good connection with the prospect, the follow-up process begins. I call this the *Forever Follow-up* method. It means we will follow-up with each prospect from now until the end of time.

While I've stressed the importance of phone calls and face-to-face contact, Forever Follow-up requires regular emailing. Once your contact list has grown to hundreds or even thousands, time limits require a reliance on email for follow-up. So be sure you get each person's email address. This way you can put them on your weekly, bi-monthly or monthly market reports.

The exact frequency of your email reports will be your call. Find out what your clients want. Some markets need weekly information. Some clients want bi-monthly or monthly. Ask clients and find what works best. Once you decide how often your report will go out, commit to it. Send it out with regularity—forever. Make sure it is sent out on the same day every single time. This will show structure and dependability. When they see this report on the same day, every time, they will start to respect you as a trustworthy, hard-working professional.

Regular, Concise Reports

So, once potential clients have given you their email address, you immediately place them on your list of people who will receive your reports. Now make sure your reports are worthy of their attention: **short and sweet, but with great insight and info about the market**. Include recent closed sales, new listings, any breaking news about the market or area, plus self-promotion of your own recent listings and sales. Draw a different picture every week that will bring attention to each report.

Get as many email addresses as you can and start sending out reports. Any prospect you talk to about buying or selling in your market, as well as your sphere of influence, should be added to this group. This will be your foundation of marketing that keeps everyone you have ever encountered in the loop with the market and with your success. If you ever fail to hear from a prospect for a long period of time, but still have their email address, keep them on the list. They may yet come back to you years later because they never stopped getting your reports. Because email is free and quick, it is a great way to stay in touch with hundreds of people that you couldn't stay in touch with otherwise.

But of course, email is not a panacea, not an "end all-be all." If anything were to be described as that, it would be the telephone.

The bottom line is that following up with prospects is something that continues forever. To recap: once you come in contact with them, get all the contact information you can get from them. Send them emails and reports on a regular basis, mail-outs (letters/postcards) every month, and make occasional phone calls… until the end of time.

Of course, most of your calls every day will consist of hot leads you need to follow-up with and new prospects you want to pursue. Besides new and hot leads, the other groups that need occasional phone calls are Sphere of Influence contacts and past clients. These guys all need attention. Schedule days specifically to reconnect with your Sphere and any past clients. You can never predict when a past client will decide to pursue another real estate deal. They may have just moved into their new dream home, saying they will be there forever, but suddenly inherit money and want to buy a vacation home or an investment property. Anything can happen. Check in with them and see how they are doing and ask if there is anything you can do for them. Go deeper with these relationships. Ask them what their plans are in real estate and who else they know that may be interested as well.

If you haven't noticed, the advice in this book is focused around outworking your competition, connecting with past clients and future potential prospects. It's the name of the game. Once you understand that it's a numbers game (i.e. the number of people you connect with dictates the number of closings you have every month), then the "path is math." And "mind over matter." I'm not just throwing cliché's and catch phrases at you; when I use these phrases and principles, it is because I've tried them, and they work… but only if you put these principles into your philosophy and into practice.

You can achieve all your goals in life by adjusting your attitude, decision-making skills and time management. But it's all up to you. Nobody on God's green earth will do it for you. Your future success falls on your shoulders alone. If you fail, you are the only one to point a finger at. Don't disappoint yourself. Make your sales calls. Connect with your customers. Then create financial freedom for yourself and your family.

Concentrate on the actions that create and nurture relationships with the people who buy and sell property within your niche market, and follow-up forever.

Chapter 12: Leverage Your Listings

Speaking of cliche's: when I began, the first real estate catch phrase I heard was that you must *"List to last."* Sayings become cliché's because they are usually **true**. "List to last" means that if you can't list property for good prices on a regular basis, you will not last in this business. This is usually true. As they also say, "the exception proves the rule." The exception is that I *do* know an exclusive buyer's agent who does very well... but I only know *one* of them. The chances of succeeding are extremely low without becoming a great Listing Agent. Look at the most successful agents in your market and around the world, all of them are primarily agents who focus on Listings. These agents work differently, talk differently and think differently than the large percentage of agents who fail to succeed before throwing in the towel. Most successful agents have a "Listings first" mindset. They live by the "List to last" rule.

Once you have committed to the Listing business, made your connections and started your forever follow-up, now it's time to get more listings. Once you have gained the trust of an owner and you have established a working relationship, listen for the opportunity to ask for the listing. They may tell you exactly and clearly that they are ready to list, or they may offer a vague, less-committed indication that they are *almost* ready to list. If they do flat out tell you they are ready to list and they want you to be their agent, then great. Get the paperwork together and make it happen.

If your potential client starts hinting around about it, but act like they can't make up their mind or pull the trigger, it may be a good time to say, "I feel like we should just go ahead and get it on the market." **Try not to use the word *listing* or *listing agreement* or *contract*.** Most sellers don't respond well to these words because of past experiences with other agents. Using the phrase, "Get it on the market," is far more positive. Once that is agreed to, then refer to the listing agreement as the *paperwork* or *price agreement*. This will go over more smoothly.

So, don't ask for the listing too early. Matter of fact, don't ask for much of *anything* too early. Have patience. Usually the first time you talk to a new prospect, the goal is merely to connect and stay in contact. Follow the sequence I mentioned in a previous chapter: ask to stay in contact, then ask for their email address and other contact information, then wait on asking for the listing and other business questions only after you know that they feel comfortable with you. The first step is to stay in touch and let them know that you are ready to help them buy or sell at any time.

Sometimes they will tell you when they are ready and other times you will capitalize on the deal only if you directly ask for the business. This takes intuition and judgment. And you won't win them all. But if you do your job by staying in touch with enough prospects, you will stay busy listing and selling property. Patience is a virtue. Start relationships and stay in touch. While you are waiting on those relationships to blossom into transactions, use that time to start new relationships, multiplying your time. Have faith and be optimistic.

Seller Motivation

Finding a seller's motivation to sell is a major step toward listing property. The motivation of the seller will tell you many things about the direction of the deal. It will tell you if they *need* to sell or would *like* to sell. There is a big difference. If a seller **needs** to sell mainly because they need the cash, then price is less important and speed of sale is more important to them. If they **want** to sell, you then ascertain what factors are involved in that.

You never know what a seller's motives are until you ask. If a seller would like to sell because they think the time is right for profit on their property, price is more important to them. These are the type of sellers who say they don't *have* to sell, but will if they can get the right price. If their price is too far above the actual current market value, you must decide if you want to take the listing or not. Sometimes it's better to tell them that they are unrealistic and to wait until the market improves. Or you can decide to take the over-priced listing with the game plan that the seller will eventually become more realistic, and/or the market will improve over time, and together you will find a middle ground.

Accepting most of these types of listings is usually fine if you can explain to the seller that "it may be overpriced but I'm happy to give it a try." Another facet of this is when the seller doesn't have to sell, but would like to only if they can get their price, *and* their price is inline or close to the current market. This is a great situation to be in. They will price it right and are not in a hurry to sell. Perfect.

As stated earlier, the single most important question you can ask a seller when looking for motivation is, *Why are you selling?* Use this question to start the conversation about why they are selling and what they will be doing once they do sell. Embark on a journey with them about this. Take the time to go deep and ask more questions pertaining to their situation and objectives.

Once we confirm that a prospect is ready to put property on the market, it is our job to price it right and create a great presentation for MLS. When pricing listings, you should keep it as close to the closed sale prices of comparable properties, otherwise known as the *comps* for the subject property. The comp prices are what the buyers will base their offers on and the appraisers will base their appraisals on. Regardless of what price the seller thinks their property is worth, it is vital that they understand what the realistic market value is in the current market area.

Servicing your Listings

Once you get the listing, it's time to start servicing the listing. This involves two important activities:

•Efficiently handling the showing requests when other agents want to show the listing, and

•Staying in close touch with the owner about the showing activity, and sharing prospective buyers' feedback after the property is shown.

You must do these two things in a timely manner with a high degree of proficiency. Without these two ingredients, your business and reputation will deteriorate. You see, when you take a listing, the owner is depending on you to be on top of every situation on his/her behalf. And they expect you to report everything you can back to them. Don't let these responsibilities overwhelm you. All you have to do is put smart systems in place.

My system is to have my assistant handle all of the showing requests, and I make it a point to talk to all of my listed owners every week or two to update and touch base with them. My assistant handles all the calls and messages from other agents who wish to show one of our listings to one of their clients. This takes most of the pressure off of me. As far as staying in touch with the owners, I prefer to do that myself. An owner listed their property with me for a reason, because they want to deal with *me*.

As I've said in this book and my previous one, real estate is about *relationships*. Therefore, I want to make sure they are getting what they want, which starts with personal contact. This is the same reason that I do not have a team. I feel like a team will water down and dilute customer service. My clients want to hear from me because of my experience and market knowledge... not from a new agent who I might be training. I take all the time most agents spend trying to build a team and concentrate on my clients and what their needs are.

Listings are Gold… If You Leverage Them

We've seen the value of multiplying efforts. Leveraging is similar: you move one lever and it multiplies your strength to lift something heavier. Listings should be multiplied and leveraged! **Each listing you get should be viewed as three potential deals for you:**

1. You should **sell the listing**. Obviously, that's immediate and significant income.

2. You should receive at least one **Buyer Lead** just from having that listing—a lead that you can refer out if you so choose, or develop yourself when appropriate. Listings attract buyers.

3. **This yields that.** Through obtaining and selling this one listing, you can use this credibility in the market to find another listing in the same area.

These are the three deals that you should start working on the second you get a listing. Leverage your listings by three, instantly.

As soon as I get a listing, I call all the surrounding owners and let them know about it. I find out if they might be interested in my new listing, and if they say "No," I use the Magic Questions (see 8) to create the relationship and get their email address. This will boost your name brand in the area as a local specialist, bringing more clients into your pipeline.

If you have a sign placed on the property, you may receive "sign calls" from drive-by buyers. Treat these seriously. Remember, each person who calls saying, "I saw your sign" may be a potential buyer for one of your listings (maybe not even the property where the sign was posted) or a potential seller. Go after them and see where it goes. An incoming call is a "hot lead" who cost you nothing in time and money. That incoming call required no time investment on your part, so treat them well. If it turns out they are not serious, don't waste much more time—refer them out.

Every listing you get goes into the MLS and is distributed through all the syndicated real estate websites, such as *Trulia* and *Zillow* (two of the largest amongst many others). Since you already have your MLS-system membership, this happens for free and thus could bring you free buyer leads. Take these and immediately put them into your email database, and then follow up with them. Find out what their situation is and how you can help them. Refer them out if necessary. Just don't ignore them.

A Listing is a Reason to Make Contact

Use all angles you can think of to leverage contacts when you get a listing. Having the ability to get a listing makes your mark on the market. Take advantage of it. Send a postcard or letter to the other owners in the area. Put the new listing on your email market report. Follow up with other buyers you have been working with recently and let them know about it. Use the listing as a reason to contact people. While making contact, use that opportunity to create a lifelong relationship.

Even at the risk of repeating myself, I cannot overemphasize the importance of nurturing relationships. Top producers connect with more than 90% of their prospects. Top producers turn almost every listing into three-fold fruit. And top producers do this by maintaining relationships. This is a trait that you should always work to improve. Getting along with people and finding something you both relate to will be key to your success.

Creating and maintaining relationships is what this business is all about. Without it, you are dead in the water. If you can become great at relationship-building, and continue to do so at a high level, you will achieve your dreams and beyond. Work the numbers and find motivated sellers who want to work with you. There are plenty of them out there. It's up to you to put in the work to find them.

Go get 'em!

Chapter 13: Hire an Assistant

In my first book, *Zero to Diamond: Become a Million Dollar Real Estate Agent*, I shared the correct procedure for finding and hiring the right assistant. I'll ask again: When you are new to the business, how do you know when it's the right time to hire an assistant? My answer is still the same: I realized I needed an assistant when I got to **thirty listings**. This was my breaking point (yours could be different) at which I could no longer handle all the showing requests, and needed to concentrate on my core business—without reducing the number of showings. Since I couldn't clone myself, I sought an assistant.

I put ads out seeking an assistant, asked colleagues for candidates, and then narrowed the list down using the method I shared in the previous book. I found a superstar assistant, and that has been a huge part of my success. I would succeed without an assistant, but I would never have come close to reaching the highest levels of production I've attained. It is very rare for a realtor to consistently gross millions, or net six figures, without an assistant. My current assistant has been with me for over three years as of the writing of this book. Her name is Krystie. She keeps the Ricky Carruth train rolling... so Thank You, Krystie, for all you do!

Finding the right assistant is not easy, but once you find one, your business and life will change dramatically in very positive ways. The problem I see with most agents is that they try to hire an assistant too early. For one thing, they can't afford one yet. Second, a new agent is not knowledgeable enough yet to truly train and fully utilize an assistant. Third, they are hiring an assistant for the wrong reasons. They are hiring them because they don't want to work too hard and they feel like hiring an assistant will wash away all their problems. If one's problems are rooted in personal laziness, no staff can clean that up.

If you hire an assistant too early, you will not know how to properly train them because you are still in the learning stages of the business. It would be like a brand new National Park Ranger hiring a brand-new trail guide when neither of them know anything about the park's trails. It would be the lost leading the lost, except that in the realty business, *you* are the one paying the blind guide's salary!

The correct stages in building a real estate business is first to work as an agent with no assistant for as long as possible so you can fully understand the business, while saving money. You should learn every aspect of the business from the inside out. Using this approach will strengthen your skills and your entire business from top to bottom. Being in the business for at least several years first will prepare you better to train your assistant once you decide to hire one. What's more, if your assistant ever goes on vacation or has to take maternity leave or sick leave, you will know what to do in their absence.

The timing of exactly when to hire an assistant will be different for each realtor. My threshold was thirty listings. Yours may be ten, or it could be forty. Assuming you have read, understood and accepted my cautions in this chapter, you will know when the time is right. If I had to advise you in a sentence, it would be this: Hire an assistant only when it would cost you more, in lost business, to NOT hire one. Another measure is when your non-dollar activities are holding you back from completing your productive, dollar-making activities. The problem is that even though the dollar activities are make you more money, the non-dollar activities still must be done and are just as important in the whole scheme of things. Therefore, it's important to find an assistant who can handle these activities efficiently and professionally.

Recognize where you are in the journey of your career. Are you still learning? Are you getting close to needing an assistant? Do you overwork? And if you have hired an assistant, are you sure that they are the best fit for your business? Constantly ask yourself where you are in the journey and what you can to do get better and become more efficient. Then hire accordingly.

Chapter 14:

Maintain a High Level of Production

As I said, there is no such thing as "The Top." In the beginning of your career, you may have set certain goals thought you defined as being at the top. However, later in your career, after you have worked very hard and given it all you have to achieve your goals and get to the so-called top, you may realize that it was just a mirage. The top disappeared, to be replaced by another mountain to climb. This is the moment you see everything much more clearly. You find out that the top is no different than the bottom. Today I am just as motivated and just as hungry as my first day in business. I'm trying to get better always. Each day I feel like a new agent looking for the best way to succeed.

Being the best may be a goal that motivates you. Having lots of money for the freedom and the material things it offers may motivate you. Or you may be more motivated by being in a position to use wealth to make a difference in the world, to help others. Finding your "why" will help you operate at your full potential and keep you motivated during the harder times.

In real estate and life, there are ups and downs. If we didn't have the lows, we wouldn't appreciate the highs. So be grateful to be in the situation that you are in. Know that it can all be taken away from you in the blink of an eye. Don't take anything for granted, and live life to the fullest.

As you work hard every day to attain your dreams and goals, you will hit times when you feel like your life and business are stalling out. I call this plateauing. Your success shot up and then started to flatten out. It doesn't matter what you do, you just can't seem to get to the next level. One problem is unrealistic expectation. Your mind can play tricks on you. Most people *overestimate* what they can accomplish in 6 months to a year, but far *underestimate* what they can accomplish within a 5 to 10-year time frame. So, monitoring expectations is one thing to consider as objectively as you can.

When I plateau, that is when I reach for something motivational: a book, a coach, a video—something that will sharpen my skills and keep me moving in a positive direction. I like to listen to audio books using Amazon's "Audible" books phone app. You can download just about any book imaginable and start listening to it immediately. Do this when you are driving form place to place. Turn your vehicle into a university on wheels. I also like certain podcasts. Reach out to me and I will suggest some really good books. I also counsel with several high producing agents and friends who keep me in a positive, upward direction.

I have also hired several real estate coaches in my career and I am here to tell you that good ones are worth every penny. Every agent gets something different out of a coach. Some need a coach for learning the fundamentals of real estate. Some need them for the accountability. And some need it more for attitude and proper mental state. I highly recommend using a coach if you have the opportunity. The money you spend will be made back very quickly if you follow their system. Motivation leads to making money.

Are You Selfish?

Speaking of money and of striving for the highest levels of profit, let me answer this question: "Is it selfish to make lots of money?" The answer should be obvious: only if you don't use that money to help others. However, we first have to make the money before we can share the money. We have all heard the saying, "You have to help yourself before you can help others." But that does not mean to stop at helping yourself, at only building your own success. You must do both: establish yourself as a success SO that you can also help others. This is the secret to life and happiness. **My goal in life is to help others.** I got into real estate to help others. I am writing this book to help others. I give to many different charities, including The Children's Miracle Network, from every single commission check I receive.

Doing these things and living life this way is extremely humbling and rewarding. It gives me a reason for what I do. I understand that people who do not know me could look at me and say that I am greedy, and that I am all about the money. This is so far from the truth. If I had not worked my fingers to the bone for decades to get where I am, there is no way that I could help anyone. If I were unsuccessful, I couldn't help myself, my family, my friends or my co-workers. Therefore, I saw it as my duty to succeed. I had to be money-conscious in the beginning to get to a point where I could start giving back. Most people are too nice and don't understand the importance of helping yourself first, then having the ability to help others. The more successful you are, the more people you can help.

Agents who are unsuccessful and are not willing to make phone calls may be, in their own way, *selfish*. Yes, I said it. Here's why: at some point, they heard that making cold calls is a good way— probably the fastest way—to succeed in real estate. And they know that if they became successful, then they could help all of those around them (friends, family, co-workers, and everyone around the world). But, because they can't handle the little bit of discomfort in first starting to cold call strangers, they decide providing for their family and helping others is not as important. To me, that's selfish.

We are all selfish in one way or another. And in one sense, isn't being unsuccessful another form of selfishness? Not making the extra effort to become a success limits how much you can do to help other people. You owe it to everyone, and to yourself, to succeed.

When agents fail in this business, it is almost always because they didn't want it bad enough and were unwilling to talk to enough people. I know this sounds like I am being harsh, but this is something I needed to say in good faith, so that I am giving you everything that I can to help you become successful. That's what I would want from you if the roles were reversed.

Chapter 15: Live the Diamond Life

In my first book, I included a chapter with this same title, "Live the Diamond Life." I discussed the importance of recharging your batteries by not working yourself to death (except during your initial business start-up), eating right and exercising. All of which are extremely important. You must have that work/life balance. I also pointed out the reason for the title of the book. The Diamond Award is a RE/MAX award given to agents who have personally grossed more than $1,000,000 in commission within one calendar year. These facts are very important and each one needs to become part of your life-map. However, don't get caught up in a cycle of spending too much attention on any single area. If you work out more than anything else, you may be in great shape, but then could be lacking in the financial department. Or vice versa. And the most obvious: if your life only consists of work, you will eventually burn out. So, refer to the first book for more details on life balance and how that plays into your business.

In this book, I want to take the Diamond Life a step further, going deeper into what the end game is all about. Through the process of writing my first book, staying motivated to write it while still juggling a huge real estate business, I learned one of the great secrets to life. My motivation to get into real estate, write these books and wake up every morning is and always will be **to help others**.

Yes, I originally got into real estate, in part, to earn a living, but also with the full intention to help people buy and sell property. I viewed the entire business differently than some: I wanted to help. So, once I finally made my first sale after eight long months in the business, I had learned how to help one person sell a property. After I sold the first one, it was like dominoes falling. I sold two a month for a few years. As soon as I started getting the hang of it, the national economy tanked and my regional real estate market crashed. I lost everything. And when I say everything, I mean everything. I didn't have a transaction for three years. However, I never gave up. I just had to recalibrate and recommit.

I eventually started selling foreclosures to buyers. That was my foot back into the market. I learned my lessons from the Crash, which was: 1. Never give up, and 2: Create lifelong relationships with every client you have. Since learning that lesson, my business has grown by leaps and bounds each year. This is when I finally realized that helping others was not about the transaction, or even real estate for that matter. It was about the right way to approach life in general, and specifically within my business, to strive for lifelong relationships, helping people in any and every way I could— forever. Once I realized this, the sky was the limit for me... and still is. Every day is just like my first day in business, where I ask: "How can I get better?" I push myself every day to learn and grow.

The bottom line is that I learned how to help people buy and sell property on a very high level.

Once you hit one level, there is always another level. No matter how high you go, there's always a step higher. This fact is something that intrigues me. It interests me. I am curious as to what the next level is and how I can get there. How many more people can I help at that next level?

For me, at this point in my career, I care about people so much and want to help so strongly that I decided to reach out and help other agents by sharing my ideas and techniques. Now that I have decided to do this, I want to do it on the highest level possible, including business counseling and one-on-one coaching, online training, speaking engagements, etc. [If you want me to come speak to the agents in your area, please feel free to reach out to me. I will be glad to do it. See my contact info in the Introduction.]

Psychologists and theologians (see Dr. Erik Erikson and Dr. James Fowler, for example) have for decades taught that the last and best stage of a person's growth and development is when they are ready and willing to teach and mentor others. This usually only happens when a person is older and wiser and more mature. But another reason for this is that until a person is financially stable and secure in their ability to care of their own immediate family, it is difficult to reach out and make sacrifices for others.

This is what I am getting at here. In the beginning of your journey to help others, you must be a little greedy, if you wish to call it that. I would call it just being hungry for success and tending zealously to the financial realities. Either way, as stated before, you can't help others until you have helped yourself and your own family first. Once you have your own house in order, then you can reach out to others with a helping hand. Be "greedy" with the right intentions, to help so many others once you reach certain levels. A person who is truly an evil, greedy person is one who steps on other people to climb the ladder of success, driven by ego to reach the top only for one's own pleasure. So, hunger and zeal are better words for what I'm talking about. Hunger and zeal are why I worked for 14 hours a day for 15 years without saying a word of complaint or boasting. I never talked about my success or bragged in any way. I kept my head down, taking massive action with a plan in mind that one day I would help so many others.

Now that I have worked so hard for so long and proved myself in the marketplace, I have the audacity to write books, create online universities and present keynote speeches. But I have been there. I have hit valleys and plateaus in my business where no matter what I did, I felt like I was going nowhere. I have had years where my profits for the year were spent, with nothing left to pay taxes. I have had doubts, worries, and feelings of rejection. I have been near the top just to have it all taken away from me right before my very eyes. More than likely, I have been everywhere you have been (or are now. So, trust me when I say that I care about you and my goal is to help you stay motivated, to not give up, to keep pushing onward and upward.

Do you have problems? Nothing fixes problems in our business better than strong production. My father always said, "Son, if you work as hard as you can every single day, all day, everything will work itself out." This might be why whenever I have gone through a hard time in my life, I would decide to just work harder. Hard work keeps my mind off whatever negative may be going on, plus I know that the harder I work, the quicker my problems will go away. So, thanks for that truth, Dad! He also said, "Son, never quit a job, just add to it." Which meant, if you don't like your current job, don't just quit; get a second job, and always keep your eyes out for a better job. This is something I still do to this day. Dad had my brother and me doing roofing when we were 7 and 8 years old. We grew up working very hard, so I sell real estate the same way I laid shingles when I roofed houses: faster than anyone around.

The moral of the story is that the secret to life is to help others. However, the best way to help the most people over the course of your lifetime is to help yourself first. When you die, it will not matter how much money you have. All that will matter is how you left your mark on this earth with the people you touched and helped. Money and wealth often follows this behavior, but more importantly, love surrounds a person with this behavior.

So... living the Diamond Life is all about a proper life/work balance and helping others reach their highest levels. Then and only then will you be truly happy.

Conclusion

Thank you so much for reading my second book. I had a lot of fun writing it. I hope that you got something out of it that you can take and use in your business and life. I am sure by the time you get this book in your hands, I will be working on a third one. If people feel like my content is helping them and worthy enough to be out there, then I will continue to create it.

The agents and readers reaching out to me about how much my first book already changed their lives has been overwhelming and gratifying. I just want to send a huge thank you to everyone who has encouraged me and shared positive words. It really means a lot and I care about everyone. Helping others is my big "Why" in life. It is what drives me. It is the reason I wake up in the morning, and the reason I keep pushing forward.

As I've stated several times, please feel free to reach out to me if there are any questions or anything I can do for you. I am extremely easy to find, easy to approach and more than willing to help. Follow me through my day on Snapchat and Instagram. Subscribe to my YouTube channel. Become a member of the *Zero to Diamond--Real Estate Agents* Facebook group, and take a look at my "online university" for my coaching clients at www.ZerotoDiamond.com. I look forward to meeting and helping you. Thanks again.

Acknowledgements

I want to give a big shout-out to my soon-to-be bride, Karlin Kaiser, the future Karlin K. Carruth. We are on a lifelong journey together and the fun is just beginning. Thank you for all your support and everything you do.

Also, thank you Dwight and Shirley Poole. Without you guys, I don't know where I would be today. Words cannot express how grateful I am for your help through the hardest years of my life.

And to my current broker, Patrick Daily (Big Daddy). I have never seen a day you were not in the best mood ever. Thank you for your positivity.

My future in-laws, Lance and Gaynor Moore. Your support means the world to me.

My grandmother, Missy Bice. You are such a warrior and inspiration to us all, and especially me. Your willingness to continue pushing forward, staying positive and keeping a great attitude is a huge reason I think the way I do.

Finally, my mother and father, Margaret Carruth and Rick Carruth. Each of you molded me in a different way that has been the perfect combination of character to dominate the world and help millions of people. I love you more than anything.

Made in the USA
Monee, IL
14 October. 2021